# GOALS

If you are uncertain, timid or vague,
If you are not sure which is the way.

If you are concerned what the future will bring,
If you are dissatisfied with any old thing.

If you are fearful of what tomorrow may be,
If you are willing to forever be free.

Then you need to take hold of your life from this day,
And you must plan a far better way.

It's goals that you need to straighten you out,
To smooth out the paths and to get you about.

For goals set a sight that is clear and is bright,
And goals give you purpose to strive and to fight.

Your life is of value and the world is your home,
So stop now and think of where you should roam.

Just make a new start, to win and to claim,
A fresh firm new goal with a definite aim.

Then chase after your goal with a desperate desire,
With passion and excellence, as if you were on fire.

Do not be timid or reluctant or slow,
Just move into top gear and let all systems go.

Copyright © 15/5/86

Peter J. Daniels,
Adelaide, South Australia

# How to reach your

# LIFE GOALS

## Peter J Daniels

THE HOUSE OF TABOR

**Other Titles by Peter J. Daniels:**
*How To Be Happy Though Rich*
*How To Handle A Major Crisis*
*How To Be Motivated All The Time*
*How To Have The Awesome Power of Public Speaking*
*Miss Phillips You Were Wrong!*

**Tutorial programs:**
*Destiny*
*How To Get More Done And Have Time Left Over*
*How To Create Your Own Dynamic Mission Statement That Works*

**All correspondence to:**
World Centre for Entrepreneurial Studies
38-40 Carrington Street, Adelaide, South Australia 5000
Telephone: (08) 231 0111   Facsimile: (08) 211 8423

**How To Reach Your Life Goals**
Copyright © 1985 by Peter J. Daniels
National Library of Australia card number
and ISBN 0 949 33007 8

The author would like to give special thanks to
Peter and Erica Haran for their valued assistance in
the writing of this book. Excellence is their style.

Printed by Gillingham Printers Pty Ltd
Adelaide, South Australia

**The House of Tabor,**
84 Northgate Street,
Unley Park,
South Australia 5061

*Dedicated to my friend,*
*Paul J. Meyer,*
*the world's master*
*goal setter.*

# Contents

# Foreword

Attaining success depends more on attitude than on circumstances. Peter J. Daniels has graphically demonstrated what can be accomplished by adopting a positive philosophy, setting challenging goals and following a plan of action for achieving those goals.

Coming from a disadvantaged background, Peter Daniels spent years in a variety of jobs and activities before he discovered the combination of beliefs and commitments that has helped him become an outstanding Christian, a fulfilled family man, a successful businessman and a millionaire property developer.

But Daniels is even more. He dreams of helping others and pursues that dream with the dedication, energy and fervor of an evangelist. He knows that what he has experienced, learned and found helpful will work for others as well. That conviction has led him to invest his time, expense and effort in sharing his experience with anyone who has a similar dream of personal fulfilment.

The road to success was not easy for Peter. His positive, up-beat approach to life came through rigorous self-analysis, unswerving faith, strong commitment and hard

work over a period of years. As an accomplished
motivational speaker, a campaigner for Christ and a lover
of excellence, Peter Daniels has found workable answers
to the universal questions about the meaning and purpose
of life. By relating his experiences and philosophy, by
witnessing for Christ and by serving others devotedly and
unselfishly, Peter J. Daniels makes easier our quest for
achievement of our full, God-given potential.

Paul J. Meyer
Founder and Chairman of the Board
Success Motivation Institute, Inc.
Waco, Texas, U.S.A.

# Introduction

This book is not a collection of other people's writings or ideas. It did not come from a desire to write or a feeling of knowledge. It is not from the high scaffolds of academia, nor is it based on ignorance. But it does come from more than a quarter-century of failures, successes, frustrations, disappointments, exhilaration, obstacles, sweat, sleepless nights and a desperate desire to achieve!

The possible difference between this book and others is that I have tried and tested every item and principle suggested. I warn you not to expect a miracle by reading this book; a miracle already has been performed by your existence. But you can fulfil a miracle by making the principles you are prepared to adopt a part of your life.

I have lectured on the subject "How to Reach Your Life Goals" around the world at the request of others. This book results from a call for additional information.

You will discover early in the book a very strange element which is rarely discussed in books on motivation. That is, success presupposes the willingness to bear pain. In understanding the implication of that, you may identify with some of the words first written by a successful man — Paul the Apostle, who said: "I pummel my body into submission."

I hope you find within these pages the spark to light your flame. I expect — even hope — that many will improve on what I have written. I have avoided wasting words on embellishment. So brevity, not verbosity, will mark these pages.

Finally, I hope I achieve my goals in writing this book by turning you, the reader, into a motivated achiever.

CHAPTER ONE

# Preparing For Life Goals

# CHAPTER ONE

# Preparing For Life Goals

**The desire**

The very fact that you have bought this book indicates that you have a desire to achieve your life goals. You exchanged your money for a purpose and you expect to realise that purpose.

This is basically true of all our actions. They are based on a desire either to gain an advantage or to avoid a disadvantage. The action of hurting or maiming another human being, for example, is normally preceded by a desire for revenge, or supremacy, or protection or gain. Even if you say you did it just because you felt like it, the desire to do it was triggered from the deep recesses of your mind. This desire accelerated your action.

Similarly, when you do something you really don't want to do, you are satisfying a desire which has probably become a habit in your life. Perhaps you are trying to avoid the consequences of something else that you are not prepared to cope with — and thus want to do even less!

It takes a certain amount of mind sifting to identify desires and to face up to the realities of the motives that stimulate them. The best way to understand your desires is to creep up on them gently, as it were. Whatever you do, do not try to meet them head on. Otherwise, you may trigger subconscious shock waves which just push them in even deeper and make the task of identifying them even more difficult — perhaps impossible. What you should do is this: casually ask yourself the question, "How far would I be prepared to go to achieve (or avoid) this goal?" Do not score a plus or minus sign against your answers, because all we are trying to establish at this stage is identification, not evaluation. If you experiment like this for a few weeks and just enjoy discovering the true depth of your desires, after a while your motives will become readily apparent.

Take care to examine your desires for false signals which may indicate hereditary or parochial habit patterns which have no real meaning to you as an individual. You need to simplify your desire profile by removing items and habits that are not really a part of you. Experience the simplicity of removing all the unwanted and heavy baggage that belongs to another time, or another person, or another place.

In creating your own value system, remember that there must be some pride in who you are and what you stand for. A cleansing at this point may prevent false starts, doubts and failures later on. You need to recognise your present desire base and keep your options open for growth within your value system. We will deal more with this subject later. In goals for life, there are many check points for discovery which will influence you, both in highlighting and expanding them.

The next step, of course, is to dig deeper, remove the desire curtain and look for basic motives. The essential skill here is to be transparently honest. We are so programmed from birth to perform to other people's expectations or codes of conduct, that we may need to ask the question, "Where do my desires really come from?"

A good measure to use in examining true motives is to ask yourself this question: *What proportion of my life am I prepared to give in exchange for accomplishing this desire?* In other words, do my desires reflect just what I would *like* to have happen or what I am *prepared to sacrifice* to have happen?

The next step is to draw up a mini-plan based on your past integrity, and your past performance with respect to both the motives behind your actions — and the things you do to protect your motives.

The questions that need to be asked here are:

1. Am I always consistent in my main mode of expression?
2. Do I use motives out of context?
3. Have my motives changed unknowingly over the years from previously set positions?

Your answers to these questions will help you assess the stability of your motives and thereby appreciate the consistency of your desire.

*Desire is the emotional thrust resulting from strong compulsive motives.* So the clearer the motive, the stronger the desire. It is of paramount importance to have clarity of thought at the motive level. This very often leads to a position of challenge with respect to how you assess a real and believable value system. It is at this level that I believe the Christian gospel with its absolute principles, provides me with the strong, deep, believable motives which give root to my desire to strive and to achieve within the boundaries with which I feel inwardly at peace.

**The will**

In my opinion, the will is the integrity of the soul. Many people who experience difficulty in exercising their willpower never get past the gritting-of-the-teeth stage. They become discouraged because of the continual failure of their willpower. As the word itself suggests, willpower is putting power into the will from the desires created by our motives. Therefore, a strong, chain effect is exhibited rather than a single decision of the will. Integrity is paramount in developing willpower. Without this honesty factor, energy is dissipated and confusion is likely to prevail.

One of the reasons we have difficulty in keeping our personal commitments is because they are just that — personal. We often over-ride a personal commitment in a way we would rarely do with a commitment made to someone else. The key here is transparency with integrity. It is something akin to an oath of allegiance to yourself. Very often the strength of commitment to the will goes hand in hand with self-esteem and self-love. You would have great difficulty in respecting anyone who continually broke commitments to you. Likewise you will not respect your own inner integrity if you break your own commitments to yourself.

I can remember someone asking me once if I had a programme to keep fit. I replied, "I get up every work-day morning and run."

"What if it is raining? Or, if it is very hot?" I was asked.

"I have made a commitment to myself," I replied, "to exercise regularly until my 85th birthday. To ask myself every morning whether the weather is suitable for me to exercise would be a lack of confidence in my integrity to fulfil that to which I have committed myself."

*You can very often do more by committing less by simply completing that which you have willed to do!* There are some simple observations which will shed light on dark areas in the mystique of willpower. Punctuality and willpower tend to go hand in hand, for instance. So do tidiness and willpower. A positive mental attitude and a strong will generally appear to be partners in life. Of course, the opposites also tend to apply. The reason I use these simple examples is that you can very often strengthen your willpower by approaching it from another angle, such as punctuality (a respect for time), or tidiness (a respect for order) or a positive mental attitude (a respect for the mind).

Other similarities may come to mind which, if you work at them, could strengthen your resolve in other areas of life. The trick is to approach it from a different angle which allows for an easing into a new routine. I call this the "side-door method." In other words, instead of trying to increase your willpower in a general sort of way, tackle one issue at a time, preferably a less difficult one. What you will find is that success in the less difficult area will help you to succeed in the other. Such habit patterns tend to strengthen your personal integrity and hence your will.

For instance, I once knew a man who had two problems. First of all, he was very much overweight. Secondly, he was never on time. He didn't seem able to overcome either obstacle. However, he began to work on the punctuality problem. He found that when he had managed to overcome this, and he was able to keep appointments on time, he also began to overcome his weight problem as well.

To play games with yourself at this stage is to put down weak foundations and the test of time will always reveal weaknesses at a later date. When the winds of life blow hard, integrity will stand, but weak structures will fall.

### Pointers
→ 1. *Accept that an act of will is an act of integrity.*
→ 2. *The will can be strengthened by using the side-door method.*
→ 3. *A decision to act is made once and vacillation only breeds weakness of will.*

### The price
*There is a price to pay for success.* In most cases, the exchange rate for establishing your commitment will

depend on your requirements. It will not necessarily be total. In fact, as each person is different in so many complex ways, it will vary from person to person. But some principles do apply.

Firstly, the cost will probably continue on a life-time basis. You yourself, and the portion of yourself you are prepared to trade with, form the basis of the exchange. This, of course, is not a new thought. Well we remember that Satan tried to trade with Jesus at the top of a high mountain. The spiritual commitment of the Saviour for the redemption of mankind far outshone the shallowness of the suggested deal.

Secondly, the price for commitment is a living thing, not a dead thing, such as money. Just by living, we are subject to variations of mood and complexities of circumstances. That is why our trade is often varied. We pay more or less for our commitment and integrity today than we did yesterday, or will tomorrow. But pay we will. There are no bad debts to be transferred. If we pay up we win: if we avoid payment, we lose. It is as simple as that. The cost is always the same in principle — and exchange of one section of life for another.

Thirdly, the bargain is binding but fair. What we exchange for our commitment-integrity are often frustration, failure, disappointment and fear. What we often receive in return are confidence, success, optimism and courage.

You may be told from time to time by others that you are on the losing side. At those times you only need to reaffirm in your mind your value system as a check point. It is possible to get off the track. So establish a pattern of affirmation to keep your objectives clear. (I will deal more with affirmation later.)

Price is the acid test of sovereignty over the will. It must establish a return greater than the original cost. This must continually activate the will and strengthen the desire when the mind and body tire and doubt creeps in. An interesting thing about paying the price for a personal pre-determined desire is that the price is virtually fixed, because you are exercising control. Conversely, if your cost is left to the elements of life, it will change like the state of one's digestion!

Of course, you will experience discomfort at times and the price may seem exorbitant against the immediate returns. But the long-term view must always occupy your focus. You must never contemplate immediate, cheap merchandise that is ill-fitting and short-lived.

In fact, when you have not made up your mind about the price you are prepared to pay in terms of time, effort and sacrifice of yourself, you will find yourself on the defensive and trying to avoid the pain level of a disciplined will. Moreover, you expose yourself to the attacks of others, not to mention factors like the prevailing economic climate, changing standards, and so on.

The Bible speaks of us renewing our minds to protect us against changing times (Romans 12:2). Within that thought is a control factor given by God to every human being. It is up to us to grasp it and use it wisely.

# CHAPTER TWO

# Assessing Your Position

# CHAPTER TWO

# Assessing Your Position

"Positioning" is a relatively new word, but its implications have been around since time began. Positioning can be a matter of accident, by being in the right place at the right time. It has to do with time, location, markets, the economy, world events, shortages and gluts. It has no particular sign or label, but its fruit abounds almost everywhere and almost all of the time. Just as a football match has sections of the field in full flight a large percentage of the time, so does life — and the ball goes to the best positioned player.

You can position yourself by studying trends, markets and generally recognising hidden opportunities.

Good positioning comes from recognising three simple rules.

1. *Make sure you are the initiator.* This does not mean you always have to be first, but it does mean you should recognise that somewhere in the cycle of events a unique opportunity exists where you could provide a service or alleviate a problem. The key is to recognise change, or pending change, and shift yourself accordingly to act as a pivot point. Set this task as a life pattern so that goals can

be reached by using your position.

2. *Maintain control in every situation.* You are most of all responsible to yourself. To neglect that responsibility will finally render you impotent to assist your fellow man. Often we lose control through the fear of missing out on an opportunity, and on other occasions we may lose control when a situation becomes desperate and the axe is about to fall. Control is essential, it enables you to take advantage of a crisis rather than be disadvantaged by it.

3. *Do not be greedy.* I have seen more people fail to succeed, or, suddenly crash after succeeding, through greed than through any other factor in life. There is a quick way to measure your greed factor by simply asking yourself the question: "If I sold now, would there be something left for someone else?" You should be able to answer "yes." Make a point of always leaving something for someone else if you have done well out of a project. Remember, the person you do not need today, often becomes the ally of tomorrow.

The final point to remember on personal positioning is: in this shifting world keep placing yourself in the corner in which you want to operate. Avoid suspicion and over-caution — such traits can paralyse you with fear and doubt. I believe God placed us here on Earth in a position of time and space. It was no mistake. It also was full of possibilities, so we should follow through and adopt the perfect position to achieve life's goals.

### Pointers
→ 1. *Make sure you are the initiator.*
→ 2. *Maintain control in every situation.*
→ 3. *Do not be greedy.*

### Family positioning
The family into which you are born is possibly one of the most important positioning aspects of your life. There are the fortunate born into wealth, prestige and power.

The less fortunate are born into poverty and a traumatic family environment.

My own background provided definite limitations, but as I became older, I learned that the family I was to develop, with my own wife and children, was far more important and therefore far more influential in my family positioning than I could ever have imagined.

You can create, under the hand of God, the kind of family environment you want and are prepared to pay the price for. This will reflect your own values and aspirations, which gives an affirming effect on your positioning, as well as providing a family positioning springboard for your children.

I am not talking here about social status so much as ethical and attitudinal status. If you maintain a high ethical standard in your family, then everyone in the family wins, along with the community as a whole. A great deal of my early career was spent undoing attitudes and ethics which held me back, and most of my time counselling others today relates to locked-in ethical and attitudinal behaviour traits which need to be dismantled and replaced before success can be obtained.

**Social positioning**

Social positioning is a choice in my opinion, and provided respect and honesty prevail, one stratum of society is no better than the other. You can be super-successful on any level, but you are wise to select where you are going to be most comfortable in relation to your desires and personality. Be prepared to make changes if required. The key is manoeuverability — develop the ability to fit into any level and accept people where they are and how they are. In doing this, watch your positioning expand its boundaries and widen opportunities for yourself. Remember, you can change your position temporarily or permanently. You only have to work at it and give it time.

A study of etiquette will allow you the freedom of knowing the right thing to do and will give the confidence required for most situations. Another factor is that social positioning also limits and locks in one's influence. A well-rounded social structure is of more benefit than staying with one executive group and thus not benefiting from exposure and opportunities at different levels. Someone once said, "Be nice to people on your way up —you meet the same people on the way down!"

## Positioning by experience

Much of what you are today is a result of past experience, and this can often lead to a claustrophobic feeling; your position is somehow "locked in." This is simply not true — experience is in the past and it can stay there. *I contend it is never too late to change.* The secret to making use of past experience is selectivity. Do this: examine carefully and objectively the effects of past experiences upon you — the good and bad, recent or distant. Write them down and study them.

Generally you will find past experiences will have had a suppressive effect on your life and act as danger signals to prevent painful recurrences. It is the bad experiences we lock away — consciously or subconsciously — and many people will fail in life as those memories linger on. It is necessary at this stage to take a closer look at the subconscious, which includes the imagination, if we are going to become goal-setters.

The subconscious is either a powerful ally under control, a machine left in neutral, or an enemy out of control, regurgitating bad experiences. If you are serious about performance and quality in life, continued effort is essential in identifying problem areas of experience. Seek out fact from fiction, replay past events in your mind and seek the benefits from each event. Now you can programme the good and dispense with the bad.

Any business that is worth its salt has a company policy

based on good and bad experience input. Develop your own personal policy for growth by documenting both clear guidelines that you know have helped you in the past and things to avoid which have caused you anguish. Remember to look for good always, because your imagination will usually pick up the disaster areas and the subconscious will readily absorb them as real experience which will influence your future output.

## Pointers
→ 1. *You can create under the hand of God the kind of environment you are prepared to pay the price for.*
→ 2. *Develop the ability to accept people where they are and how they are.*
→ 3. *The secret of making use of past experience is selectivity.*

## Positioning by education
Who has not felt the limiting factors of our education? The more we learn, the more we realise there is to learn. The real question that needs to be addressed is, "Do I understand the simple principles of life and comprehend its flow?"

I am forever receiving letters of request from mediocre performers for updated information on new and highly specialised psychological and learning advances. There appears to be a misguided idea that "the more advanced information I can collect, the more successful I will become." Educators in general have encouraged this ill-founded and unproven philosophy to the point where an army of "information gatherers" has developed.

Look into the life of your nearest friend or acquaintance who is successful and you will discover that, whether schooled or unschooled, they use the education they have to the fullest extent and continue to build upon that education in line with present and future goals. But rarely will such a person gather information which is neither practical nor useful.

*Education is expandable and changeable and should be adaptable.* It is useless to set goals in one direction and then to waste valuable time and energy expanding your knowledge on something else. Assess where you are now as far as your education is concerned, and then evaluate what you need to know to get where you want to go. Set your sights on acquiring information as a tool to get the job done.

### Pointers
→ 1. *Don't be a wasteful "information gatherer."*
→ 2. *Remember you can change your education direction.*
→ 3. *Always seek to expand your education in line with the way you are going.*
→ 4. *Seek out practical information relating to your needs.*

### Success
In assessing your present position, be fair with yourself, particularly in regard to past successes. Nobody has failed at everything. Those successes you have had can be used as building blocks. Count them up and evaluate how you won the day. Was it luck, timing, special knowledge, hard work, risk or information? Now write it down; log those things you have done well and be generous with yourself.

As a success-oriented person remember *success is not a dirty word.* It is mentioned in the first chapter of Joshua and is further encouraged throughout scripture (Josh 1:7,8; 1 Chron 22:13; 2 Chron 20:20). Keep in mind too that man was created to subdue the earth and have dominion over it (Genesis 1:27,28), which gives us a sovereign charter for growth and achievement and no room for contemplation of failure.

Success is for you because humanity itself strives always to win, to obtain, to overcome and to possess. Every new-born baby emphasises that hope and promise. Every new step taken by a young child illustrates success and accelerates the youngster on to greater achievement.

Success is for you because God committed it to your development within the confines of the biblical charter. You were created, programmed and given opportunities to succeed and the responsibility is now yours. Success means total responsibility in:

1. *My planning*
2. *My development*
3. *My achievement*
4. *My failures*
5. *My behaviour*

These demonstrate a personal growth, a commitment to others and a respect for truth. This will lead us to our ultimate potential.

## Failure

At one time or another we all have felt the helplessness of despair and failure. An old-timer once said, "You don't learn anything from the second kick of a horse." This ought to be true, of course, but for most of us it takes three or four kicks before things start to sink in!

I remember my first business failure. After the humility and disappointment, I was feeling very sorry for myself, but I soon came to the unmistakable conclusion that the fault lay directly within myself. The evidence for this was quite clear! Other people were running similar businesses with similar restraints and difficulties, but they were successful. It was painful to accept the clear hard fact that my frivolous attitude towards money was the real problem.

The second time I went broke was because of my sloppy attitude to keeping proper records and not clarifying one step before moving on to the next.

The third time I failed was because I was chasing a dream without removing the nightmares that can be experienced by over-estimating my own ability and leaning too much upon other people.

Out of all such experiences, lessons can be learned. Assess your present position and provide the foundation for setting your goals. Do not overlook the lessons learned from failures and certainly do something to rectify weaknesses, but *keep your eye always on the lesson learnt, not on the destructiveness of failure.*

And learning lessons is what failure is — or should be — all about. During one period in my business life I could not put a foot right for five years straight. My wife said, "Give up and work for someone else."

I said, "Never! God knows what a stubborn fool I am and He is teaching me a lesson." I found out if you keep failing over the same things, you will never graduate, because you have not learnt the lessons properly. It is as simple as that. If you do make the same mistake twice, examine it in close detail, learn a lesson and don't forget it.

Another point worth noting is: *don't break well-learned principles.* You do so at your peril, as my son Graham once found out. He lost an enormous amount of money and after 18 months struggle I asked him what lessons he had learned. He said, "In future I will maintain control." Control — a life principle.

### Pointers
→ 1. *Don't let failures crush you — remember failures are lessons.*
→ 2. *Having the same failure twice rarely teaches you anything new, it just emphasises the lesson.*
→ 3. *Document your lessons into life-principles to prevent recurrence.*
→ 4. *Overcoming failure builds character and it is a ladder to success.*

→ 5. *Failing in life is like failing in school — you don't go up to the next grade until you've learned your lesson.*

## Exposure

Exposure is important because, by exposure we get experience, and with the experience comes valuable knowledge. Timid minds never venture into the world of exposure. However, timidity can be overcome by realising that in accepting mentally the results of the worst that can happen, we use that as the instigating force to do our best to make sure it doesn't happen.

*Remember — nothing is as final as it seems at the time.* Businesses can be rebuilt, broken bodies healed. Even damaged or destroyed reputations can be resurrected and financial security can be regained. There is an abundance of evidence in every city or town where someone has overcome simply by being prepared to enter into the arena one more time. This means, of course, more exposure, more risk, more experience and thankfully more knowledge.

Avoiding exposure is like trying to become proficient at riding a bike without getting on it! You have to mount it and have a few falls and near misses to become accomplished at riding it. So is the principle of life's progress. You have to expose yourself to danger, failure, embarrassment and ridicule sometimes to achieve security, success, confidence and esteem.

I am not suggesting you ignore sound advice, but I am urging you to be bold in exposure, so that in the future, you may have the recall to form opinions, create confidence and apply principles learned.

Particularly try to seek exposure in situations where you can gain experience at little or no cost. Expose yourself by accepting an official position in your club and, by that exposure, gain experience dealing with people. Help with the finance campaigns for your church or charity or the political party of your choice. Offer to debate subjects or volunteer to help at working bees. Take on an extra risk at work and stay a little later to become proficient at something new. Try a new sport, or go camping in the wilderness. Learn to ride a horse, or water-ski. Acquire an agency for a saleable product and learn to market it, or make something to sell. Confront a person who has been bullying or harassing you. Build your exposure ratio as another foundation stone towards your support system for accomplishing your life's goals.

### Pointers
→ 1. *If you are without exposure, you are without experience.*
→ 2. *Gain exposure and gain inexpensive experience.*
→ 3. *Confront situations to strengthen resolutions.*

CHAPTER THREE

# Recognising Your Personality Strengths

# CHAPTER THREE

# Recognising Your Personality Strengths

**The people person**

In preparing your life's goals, try looking into yourself as a person a lot deeper than you are now. Analyse your personality because this is essential in programming your life. Stand back and take a look at yourself and accept that a personality can, in fact, be developed in various areas to suit the goal needs.

Take first *the people person*. He is the one who loves to gather with people; he immensely enjoys the company of others and you can recognise him at any get-together. His behaviour shows as he moves from one group to the next. Generally, he is the last to leave. When he does depart, he has usually made arrangements to meet someone at a later date.

The people person, you'll find, is the one who remembers names, recalls events and previous meetings. This is because he is intensely interested in people and is well-liked by others.

I am not a people person. To this day I would be happy living in isolation, thinking, reading, writing and enjoying my own company. But I had to change my personality to become gregarious, develop conversational skills and get on with people. I had to do this quite simply because it was part of achieving my life's goals. Goal-setters are people persons due to a God-given principle — we are part of a giant family of mankind, we are not isolationists. We were put here to help one another.

So develop your people-person-personality, which will allow you to move in any circle, and, as a consequence, you will obtain the side effect of strengthening your own character. You will become more sensitive and compassionate as a result.

### Pointers
→ 1. *Goal-setters condition their own life.*
→ 2. *Goal-setters condition the life of others.*
→ 3. *Goal-setters remain in the mainstream of life.*
→ 4. *Goal-setters achieve life's goals.*

### The book person
A *book person* is simply one who feels confident in the reliability of the written word. I am not talking about escapism through fiction or entertainment through pleasure reading. No, I am referring to the person who is fascinated and attracted by books that develop and inspire.

However, a point to remember is that the writers of books are also human, with fears, failures and frustrations. In real life, many authors would be a surprise to their readers. I have met some authors who expose their lives clearly and confidently on the printed page, but wilt in conversation or debate.

On the other hand, there are other people who do not like reading, and fail in debate when confronted by someone with a deep knowledge of written facts. I used to avoid reading with the usual excuses of lack of time, inability to concentrate and something of a lack of comprehension. But then I found my mind was like a muscle. Do enough push-ups and it will expand and absorb and become flexible. Surely, I reasoned, if I read enough and expanded my vocabulary, I would enjoy reading and reap the benefit. It still amazes me what a truism this is. My life has expanded through reading, more than I dreamed possible.

Make it a practice, if you are a book person, to be with people more often. Ask them questions about themselves, their families and interests; become more public and take a higher profile. Conversely, if you are not a book person, you have cut yourself off from a valuable source of knowledge. Both a people person and a private person can expand their horizons by reading applicable material.

## Pointers
→ 1. *Do not substitute books for people.*
→ 2. *You may know it in theory; do you know it in practice?*
→ 3. *Tune into other people's experience.*
→ 4. *You can build reading and concentration skills.*

## Style
Every one of us has style, that indefinable quality which gives us the stamp of individuality. It is very much an outward quality. We may be gruff, noisy, quiet, explosive or flamboyant. Style is what you do and the way you do it. What we are looking for here is a style which will help us achieve life's goals. To take some examples. If we are seeking to become the best undertaker in town, playing practical jokes on people would not be a recommended style. Similarly, drinking and eating in excess will not help you become a top athlete, if that's your life goal. Have you ever met a famous person and said to yourself afterwards "that's just how I imagined him to be?" Contrast that, if you will, against an occasion when you saw behaviour from someone that was inconsistent. Interesting is it not? I am not talking here about showing off. I'm talking about

shining on — the development of flair, style, a presentation, that puts a stamp on you and makes you stand out in a crowd.

A simple example came to me when I went to stay with new friends interstate. When I entered my bedroom in their home they had a nice coloured handwritten message on the wall, "Welcome, Peter Daniels, to our home." That was part of their style. Exhibit your style when you entertain or undertake a project, or make a presentation, or introduce your friends.

When I appreciate people I usually write a poem about them and then give it or post it to them after the occasion. Can you imagine the response? Whoever has had a poem written about them in their whole life? But that's my style.

When I travel overseas I always take some Australian opals to give to people I meet. That's my style.

If I am holding a dinner party, I make sure the doorman knows by name the people who are coming, so they are greeted properly. That's my style.

If I commit myself to do something I try and go a little further. That's my style.

If I am going to promote anything, I make it a grand occasion. That's my style.

If I am going to challenge anything publicly, I make sure that my facts are startling, and correct, and publicity automatically follows. That's my style.

What about you? Do you have a style that indicates success and provokes further growth? Recognising your personality strengths and adding other strengths to them will enhance your life and increase your self esteem. Seek to obtain a balance of these three:

- A people person
- A book person
- A person with style

And then expand their usefulness to achieve your life goals.

**Pointers**
→ 1. *You can expand and develop your personality.*
→ 2. *Develop a style that is consistent with what you are.*
→ 3. *Write a description of the style you need and follow it.*

**Physical fitness**
It has been said, a healthy body reflects a healthy mind. It could also be said that if you have a healthy body, you can do what your mind requires. Physical infirmity however, reminds us of our total dependency upon God for our next step and our next breath. Therefore, in setting your life's goals, you have to pay attention to your physical inabilities, whether hereditary or accidental. I well remember in my own life suffering from rheumatic fever, diphtheria, collapsed blood cells and meningitis, and the difficulties I experienced during those dark days.

While we should not play up our infirmities, we should not ignore them either, and goals should relate to our physical condition if it is permanent. But it does not have to limit other possibilities. Paralysis may immobilise the body, but it does not immobilise the mind. A person who is physically immobile can use his brain to be a great composer, poet, inventor or a share market whiz. Infirmity in age is more of the mind than the body.

I am always amused at W. Clement Stone. When he comes to a business meeting, still in his eighties, he always greets people with the comment, "I feel happy, I feel healthy, I feel great, how about you?" Sir Bruce Small, the famous Gold Coast developer in Australia, inspired me many times, well after his 80th birthday, when he would literally run up three flights of stairs to do business.

*The key in overcoming or coming to grips with infirmity is the way you relate to it with your mind.* Life is not just a body, it is also a mind and a spirit and your physical position can either be overcome, or used as a pivot point, in attaining your goals. If you are prone to be overweight, bring it under control. If you have a particular physical weakness, always seek out the best medical science can offer and avoid situations which will irritate the condition. But do not ever confuse physical weakness with mental weakness.

Sometime ago, in our church, we were asked to pick up a lady who had recently had a minor operation on her feet. I escorted her to the car and during the ride to church, she said she didn't know how she would handle the compulsory voting in the coming federal elections. I replied, "Why don't you phone the department? They will send you the appropriate forms to fill in." After the church service, she again mentioned the matter and I responded in the same way. She came back at me again and asked me if I would phone the appropriate department for her.

I said, "No, your problem is in your feet, not in your head. You can easily do it yourself."

I remember my wife was very concerned because she thought I had spoken too harshly. But there was no need for concern because the same woman later said: "Isn't your husband wonderful? That's what I needed — someone to talk to me like that."

We need to exercise our bodies daily, pay attention to the food we eat and the sleep we get. Performance and endurance — or lack of it — can often be directly traced to poor diet and fatigue. Take note at this point, however, that we should not expect a painless life or a physical high all the time. In addition we all have our illnesses and accidents and most of us have hereditary weaknesses with which we must cope. The trick is to recognise the ups and downs, cope with them as they emerge and push ahead.

**Pointers**
→ 1. *Recognise physical defects.*
→ 2. *Do not aggravate the defect.*

→ 3. *Increase your physical fitness where possible.*
→ 4. *A weak body does not signify a weak mind.*
→ 5. *Push on regardless.*

## Concentration

Concentration can be a frustrating part of life. So often we try to concentrate on the matter at hand only to find our minds drifting off and away. I have often longed to be able to work by the sea or in a country retreat; a Shangri-la with my wife at my side. I have found out the hard way that I am a loner — I can only concentrate in solitude, without noise or interruption. I have found the depth of concentration at times like these so intense that when I am finished I am so exhausted I immediately fall asleep! *Deep concentration requires dedication, desperation and no interruptions.* Over the years I have learnt to switch off from my surroundings when the time comes to wrestle with a problem or an idea. I know that if I don't complete the concentration circle, I will lose the connection and fail to produce what I want.

In many respects concentration goes against our natural needs. Inwardly we want to be at peace and be released from pressure. Concentration disturbs both. And concentration often eludes us because we do not have a plan to reach the climax of concentration.

Try this method when you next tackle a problem requiring ultimate concentration. Firstly, formulate some headings which will require concentrated effort. Then find an atmosphere you know will be conducive to your commitment. Now set aside a time frame big enough to create what I call the "flow." When concentrating, do not get into a sleep-type posture, or think you can develop concentration by thought drift. As you may know by now, concentration is hard work, and if you do not accept that fact, you disqualify yourself.

**Pointers**
→ 1. *Accept the challenge of concentration.*
→ 2. *Realise that others have to overcome it.*
→ 3. *Prepare yourself by making headlines for concentration.*
→ 4. *Find your best concentration location.*
→ 5. *Formulate your concentration on paper.*

## Pain endurance

In the introduction to this book I spoke of the willingness to bear pain to achieve success in your chosen life's goal. The nature of man is to avoid pain, yet *pain at some level is sometimes a strong component of the achieving of goals.* Pain is a great teacher and a great preventer. The thought of pain can prevent you from acting, and the discipline of pain can make you act. Pain in its crudest form is a signal to do or not to do. But it can be much more. It is firstly a barrier that must be overcome, and in passing through the pain barrier, you can relish the euphoria on the other side.

A friend of mine who does distance running tells me that in a long distance race, when the pain is almost unbearable, he pushes on and suddenly, as if by magic, the pain vanishes and a new sensation overwhelms him, and he finishes the race. The pain of failure blights all of us with a long, accusing finger, pointing with uncanny accuracy to our omissions and fractures. Yet we must press on and endure the pain, and even learn to accept it as a friend. We must learn to interpret those crude signals although it may well be a painful experience. We will find out later in life we had to endure pain to run the race and finish the course.

Pain in learning to succeed is one thing. It almost seems a badge of honour or a diploma placed on the wall of hidden corridors in our private lives. Never think it is finished, or that the so-called diploma is a lesson taught and the graduation completed. Pain will be with you throughout your life in success and in failure, in joy and in grief. It is the ever present friend, enemy and trickster waiting in the shadows ready to pounce. It may be the pain you feel when a loved one makes a careless remark you know is not true, or a newspaper article presents you as someone you are not. It may be the tiredness you feel after an international flight when you are expected to perform at a speaking appointment in a manner worthy of a world professional — even when you can hardly stand up.

Pain occurs when you have thoroughly prepared a project, dotted the I's and crossed the T's, only to find you have been let down and the whole project crumbles. Pain occurs because of pressure upon pressure. Pain occurs when your brain feels it is about to burst if it retains one more fact or holds one more thought. There's the pain of having to hear another person talk at you and you have other people's problems overshadowing you.

But it is endurance that counts — to break through the pain barrier to a full and overflowing life. There is the aura and weightlessness you feel when the barrier is broken. It is at these times I identify with Paul the Apostle when he says, "I pummel my body into submission" and in doing so, understand the peace of God that surpasses our understanding. (1 Corinthians 9:27; Philippians 4:6, 7).

## Pointers
→ 1. *In varying degrees pain is going to be with you throughout life.*
→ 2. *Pain needs to be identified as a crude signal that may not be apparent till later.*
→ 3. *Beyond the pain threshold often awaits the prize.*

## Skills
To make a clear start on goal-setting we must recognise

our skills. Many skills are not apparent at first glance. However, we will find on close examination, that each and every one of us has inbuilt skills. Paying attention to detail may be a built-in skill; you may express yourself well verbally; you may be an excellent planner; you may handle people well or have the ability to do more than one thing at a time. Other skills are having an enquiring mind, or being endowed with patience. All of these skills are inherent or developed and can be used in a positive way to achieve life's goals. Other skills are locked away. They may appear at a time of crisis or great opportunity. Others you may have right now are being used at minimum capacity. Others are being misused. You are uniquely equipped with obvious and hidden skills, learned and gifted skills that need to be identified.

Years ago I used to call on a big store in a major country town to sell a product I was handling at the time. One day I received notice from their liquidator explaining that the company was in financial difficulties and might have to close down. They would continue for a few months to see how things worked out and they would guarantee payments of all future goods received. A strange thing happened. Orders started to come in from them again, but this time they were bigger than before. Naturally I paid them a visit only to find the most insignificant department manager was now General Manager and Chief Executive Officer and he was running the whole show. Evidently he had convinced senior management he could trade them out of their difficulties and then proceeded to exhibit skills that were not obvious before he saved the store. This man rose to full stature in a difficult situation. He had never before had the opportunity or the pressure to exert himself — and discover his skills.

You have skills, incredible skills, but you need to sharpen and document the ones which are obvious and dig deep and even put yourself into a stress situation to discover the hidden ones, if you are the least bit serious about setting and reaching your life's goals.

### Pointers
→ 1. *Identify your present skills.*
→ 2. *Provoke yourself into a situation to awaken your hidden skills.*
→ 3. *Continue to develop new skills.*

# CHAPTER FOUR

# Putting Your Life Together

# CHAPTER FOUR

# Putting Your Life Together

**Putting you together the way you would like to be**

If you had the magical power to change yourself into what you would really like to be, would you exercise that power? Of course you would. First you would have to strip away the fantasy and then you would have to get down to the nuts and bolts of what you would really want of yourself. Most people, for a number of reasons, never get past the fantasy stage. Some are not aware they really could make the change, while others are too lazy or throw up excuses and complaints as a fence and languish in comfort. After all, change requires effort.

So let's get serious for a moment and ask ourselves some hard questions, such as what if I do not even like my appearance? I cannot change that, right? Wrong.

I faced a serious problem with protruding ears that was so acute I was nicknamed "saddle flaps." I came to the conclusion one day in my early forties that I was going to correct it. I consulted a plastic surgeon and was greeted by a pandora's box of possibilities available through modern science. When I mentioned what I was going to do, a friend of mine told me it was vanity. I suggested that he take out his false teeth after every meal because that was all he needed them for — I have heard no more remarks like that! The results were incredible and the boost to my self esteem was awesome.

You can change yourself physically if you want to in a variety of ways, if you are serious and convinced that it would make a significant difference. The easiest way, of course, to change your appearance is with diet, exercise and deportment, careful grooming and clothes. If you do not understand proper fashions suitable for your lifestyle, study them. Always remember the way you carry yourself makes an incredible difference.

Many years ago I was watching a television news broadcast and I was suddenly arrested by the dress and deportment of a world leader. I then reflected on other world leaders and I began to watch the way they dressed. I noticed most international leaders dressed the same way. Most Western leaders wear blue, grey or black suits (usually in that order of preference). The suits go along with white shirts and black shoes, all immaculately put together. I made my mind up that was the way I wanted to look and to this day you will only ever see me in those colours. *Clothes may not make the man, but they certainly introduce him.*

Now let's turn to the mind. Is it presently the way you want it? Believe it or not you can change your mind because God gave you a free will; He never robotised the mind of man. Develop habit force and change your mental attitude. Correct little faults, "pull yourself up," in a manner of speaking, by your thinking habits and your attitude. The important thing to remember here is, never let an exception occur, because you will send messages to your subsconscious that you are prepared to cheat. Write down what sort of person you want to change into. It may seem that you need a magic wand — so be it. Write it down in detail and include the physical, mental and personality traits you want. And one more thing —

include your spiritual self.

By now you may realise — you do possess a powerful magic wand, it is called "choice" and it is waiting for you to press the button called "decision" to make the required adjustments in your life.

### Pointers
→ 1. *Work out the type of person you would really like to be.*
→ 2. *Detail clearly and identify on paper a full description of that person.*
→ 3. *Activate the switch called "choice" and create that person in you and within you.*

## The belief factor

The two largest stumbling blocks to a change in life are believability and mobility. The belief factor can usually be overcome by a convincing argument, peppered with facts and garnished with persuasion. Then turn your attention to mobility; get on with the job. You may now find the belief factor is again in question and a see-saw action begins, which absorbs time and energy but produces nothing.

At this stage go back to the early chapters on desire, will and price, and clear away again the accumulated debris of procrastination that prevents you from being honest with yourself and objective in your aim. Libraries of the world are full of stories of enterprises with humble beginnings, expanding into giant corporations and business empires, by insignificant people daring to do — finding they could — and becoming great. These are stories of overcoming seemingly impossible odds, using limited means, and in the end the underdog triumphs. You can be that person, you can do the task, you can expand your horizons, you can change, you can carry the load, you can overcome, you can endure, you can achieve your life's goals.

**Pointers**
→ 1. *Recognise the see-saw between belief and mobility and pass over its limitations.*
→ 2. *Re-read the earlier chapters on desire, will and price.*
→ 3. *Inspire yourself with other people's achievements and accept that you can do it.*

## Beware of the crowd

Now is the time for some warnings and mechanisms to protect against the insidious onslaughts of "the crowd." Some great entrepreneurs claim the crowd is always wrong, find out which way the crowd is heading — then consider a different direction. It takes individual commitment to assess what is right, and a crowd cannot do that. Crowds can only confirm what is right. It has been said that man in the singular is unusual and unpredictable, but that man in a group is easy to predict and evaluate. Remember you will be questioned by some about your new found ambitions, goals or lifestyles.

Never lose sight of the fact that those who question, criticise or oppose are normally part of the crowd. The crowd rarely identifies itself as such. The people concerned may not even be acquainted with one another. But you will find they clearly identify themselves by their remarks and posture. The crowd can be devious in its actions. To start with they will identify with you, even encourage you, rarely expecting you to raise your standards or achieve your goals (because they, too, had similar dreams and ambitions and in identifying with you they are stroking, as it were, their own desires). But when you begin to demonstrate growth by producing results and adding wings to your dreams, the mood changes as the crowd sees the reflections of their failures in your successes; you become a yardstick to their lives and behaviour. On the face of it, surface relationships are still intact, but be warned, there is an avalanche of criticism close at hand.

The picture becomes complete when you have achieved success. Now the crowd wants you as a friend; they are looking for the spin off and attitudes become patronising. The stance I recommend adopting is not to put down the crowd, but to be aware of the destructive nature of their actions. Crowds can absorb energy and waste time. At times, we pay too much attention to what others think of us, how they will react to our actions. Remain true to your value system and get on with the job. Jesus Christ, I am reminded, was welcomed into the city by the crowd and it was the voice of the crowd that crucified Him.

### Pointers
→ 1. *The responsibility is yours, not the crowd's.*
→ 2. *Recognise changes in the crowd, but do not be affected by them.*
→ 3. *Your life is your own, claim it.*

### Goals need form
If you were to ask any group of people, "What are goals?" you would get a number of answers — and a lot of confusion. I have tried it, and the lack of expression from some high achievers is amazing. It is not as though they are not using the goal-achieving process, their list of objectives substantiates that, but to pass that elusive quality on to others is quite another matter.

Goals are the solidification of dreams, ideas and ideals in practical form, for practical implementation for practical completion. On the other hand, dreams are elusive and grand, and away from the restraints of the pragmatic. They form the seeds of inspiration that keep our hope machine in working order. Many goals are in the twilight zone of the imagination, like smoke from a fire, real but not packageable. But if we follow its source, we will find the flame that creates the smoke.

*Goals are the result of bringing dreams, ideas and ideals*

*into tangible and examinable form.* Goals without the means to achieve are only useful for flights of fancy; an occasional pick-me-up. Without a plan we see the goals, but a section of our life is missing; we are without the bridge or mechanism to cross from fantasy to reality.

You must get your goals into written form, otherwise you will continue to play mind games which belong in adolescence rather than adulthood. I say again, get the writing habit with thoughts, quotes, expressions and ideas. Plan your dream so that you can nail down the goals and the means to achieve them. I see this as fencing them off. When you write it all down, it cannot escape from your grasp and will not become fleeting, wasted moments. I cannot stress enough the need to solidify your dreams with the written word and the need to do it quickly before the vapour of smoke vanishes and recall is lost.

### Pointers
→ 1. *Dreams are the birthplace of goals.*
→ 2. *Writing down goals assures permanence.*
→ 3. *Only solid goals can be worked on.*

### Goals need maps
Goals need a map or track to follow. I have often heard this and there certainly is an element of truth in it. Maps provide information, prevailing conditions, direction. Remember, life goals are identifiable but intangible. So we need a charted course to find the way. Our map to achieving our goals must be as explicit and clear as possible with as much detail packed in as we can manage.

Many a businessman has failed because he did not plan well, and, as the saying goes, "If you fail to plan, you plan to fail." Spend time visualising a map and the form it should take, so it will remain a clear reminder of the task ahead. I keep a small notation of my next ten years goals in my wallet as a quick reference and ready reminder so I will not stray off the track. You need a life map to the end of your life simply because that is the intelligent thing to do. The good and the bad will come along, but we move the bias towards the good because we have planned and mapped out our future. If you still have some doubt about planning your life's goals, remember God takes it even further — into eternal life.

## Pointers
→ 1. *Create a map to reach your goals.*
→ 2. *Make a list of the equipment you need.*
→ 3. *Carry a reminder with you to keep you on the track.*

CHAPTER FIVE

# Take Time To Dream

# CHAPTER FIVE

# Take Time To Dream

Day dreaming or night dreaming, pondering or purposeful thinking — all have the authority of God-likeness. The reason I make such a claim is because in any of these exercises you are developing something which was not there before in conscious thinking. Therefore, you have joined hands, as it were, with the Creator, exhibiting some of His power, validating again that you were made in His image. Why? *Because in dreaming you are creating something out of nothing.* In so doing you position yourself on the periphery of God-likeness. You become a mini-creator. Without substance or form, you create an image of an idea or event you will pursue and it will take a tangible shape. The marvellous thing about visualising, brainstorming or dreaming is — you can trigger them at will, if you keep the mechanism in working order.

Let me take that a little further. When my children were small, they would talk to me in detail about all kinds of imaginary events and present me with all kinds of imaginary things while awake, full of life and involved in adventure. In adulthood, we tend to put the brakes on our dream machine, and as we grow older, the brake is further applied until our dreaming stops. But not with great entrepreneurs. They can paint word pictures from their dreams and inspire others. I cannot resist saying here, "Do you get the picture?" Your dream machine can be turned on again by creative imagination and you can experience the wonder of the mind in a kaleidoscope of images. So take off the brake and expose yourself again to those wonders you saw as a child, but now through the strong experienced eyes of adulthood. To set your life goals, you will need to imagine your life and the world up to ten, twenty, forty, fifty years into the future, and in so doing excite your senses and reawaken your spirit to the greatness within you.

### Pointers
→ 1. *Awaken your dream machine.*
→ 2. *Dreaming is on the periphery of God-likeness.*
→ 3. *Learn to seek the full picture.*

### Too busy to dream

Some people's lives are so complicated and busy they are too busy to dream. My son, Peter Jnr., who is a director of some of our companies, said to me one afternoon, "Dad, I spent two hours alone in the lounge of the Hilton Hotel this morning imagining and dreaming and I have come up with forty new ideas." I am glad he is not too busy to dream, because if he were, he would not be successful today.

Many years ago I was faced with an uncomfortable deficit in my business and I could not come up with an idea to handle the problem. I spoke to my office manageress, Mrs. Hall, and asked her to go home and come up with an idea that would give us the extra income we needed. She said she was too busy and she could not think of anything. But I insisted and also told her to stay at home on full pay until she came up with the imaginative idea we needed! I said to her, "I know you have a simple idea and I am depending on you to deliver it." It was not long before Mrs. Hall returned with a plan, so simple it only took ten minutes to implement and provide the funds needed.

*Do not be too busy to dream, rather be busy dreaming.* Cut your heavy schedule and go alone to a quiet spot with a pen and paper or tape recorder and dream, imagine, plot, talk to yourself and think. It could be the most profitable time of the week.

Another reason some people avoid dreaming is that they are too frightened. If you develop seed thoughts into an idea and then on to a project, you have an obligation to do something about it. Then there is a challenge to our comfort zone. Dreaming is a part of life and a catalyst for the adventurous spirit. To keep it alive is to be fully alive; to dampen its fuse is to dim our lights. Goal-setters are never too busy to dream.

### Pointers
→ 1. *Slow down and dream.*
→ 2. *Do not be afraid to dream.*
→ 3. *Dreaming awakens life.*

## Spend prime time dreaming

It is not a pleasant prospect to reach a point in a hazardous journey and find you have forgotten something in your planning. Similarly, who of us in life's journey wants to reach a lofty peak only to find an avalanche of doom descending on us because we did not anticipate the inevitable? I know it is not possible to evaluate all the possibilities but not to spend prime time trying is to invite possible disaster. *Dreaming or imagining can provide us with tremendous value in paving the way.*

Let me illustrate this by telling you of the story about a pastor friend of mine who committed his church congregation to building a big new church. After the architect's plans were approved, the pastor and his church secretary took all the relevant papers up to a mountain cabin for the weekend. They laid the plans out on a large table and then did something quite unique. They had agreed to imagine the building was finished and together they would try and visualise the completed structure and "walk" inside to see if it suited their needs. The first thing they did (in their imagination) was to unlock the door and switch on the lights. When they compared their imaginative picture with the plans laid before them they found the architect had put the light switch thirty feet from the front door! Alteration number one prevented them from having to open the church with a flashlight!

Now on their imaginative tour they walked into the foyer where they wanted to see flowers or a painting on the wall. They checked the plans and found the fire hydrants were in the corridor facing the front door. Alteration number two: change the position of the fire hydrants.

So the process went on and by the end of the weekend alterations had been made improving acoustics, layout and many other aspects. This was because they spent prime time dreaming. Get into the habit and test out your projects by using the wonders of imagination.

### Pointers
→ 1. *Dreaming does not waste time, it saves time.*
→ 2. *Develop the prime time habit.*
→ 3. *Test your project by dreaming.*

### Dreaming is reality
There is nothing capricious in God's nature. This includes dreaming, because dreaming illustrates your hidden capacities and your unwakened abilities. There is no reason for God to give you the capacity to imagine and dream positively and creatively without Him expecting

you to realise the dream and complete the task. Just as you have the great power of choice to select the dream you follow, creative imagination can be directed to dream the dreams you want. But be alert to the elusiveness of your dreams and document their course, otherwise you will miss the dynamic, fleeting thought you felt so powerfully. You never expected to lose it, but if you don't secure it, you will.

I have been waiting for years to recapture a thought on a major breakthrough in behavioural science I discovered and documented (only to lose the paper and with it the recollection of those thoughts). Try as I may over many years, I have never been able to recapture its contents, although a couple of times I have felt I was on the edge of its appearing. On occasion I awaken in the middle of the night with a thought or an idea and I leap out of bed, like a man possessed, and stay up for hours writing it down. At these times, my wife will never speak or enquire, because she understands the fragility of such a moment. There have been times when I have completely forgotten about my night's events, only to discover later the evidence of my dream on the writing pad.

At one time I was particularly hard pressed for cash and I had arranged for a new product to be manufactured for sale. In my dream one night I saw another item fixed onto the unit, making it not only unique, but also more versatile and practical. The sales from that project saved the day. Dreaming is real when that sort of thing happens. Dreaming is real when you set out the direction of your dream, document its response, and then activate the plan to the end.

Do you realise your subsconscious accepts your dreams as real and, in fact, cannot distinguish the difference between a real and imaginative act? Let's assume you are asleep and you are dreaming a dream where you are in great danger. Suddenly your mouth becomes dry, your stomach tightens, your legs shake and you start to perspire, but you have not gone anywhere and nothing really has happened — or has it? Your subsconscious mind and your body act as if the situation were real. If it had really happened, your condition would not have been much different. To the subsconscious, dreaming is reality. Day dreaming and imaginings, both harmful to us and good for us, may eventually draw us like a magnet towards the subject of our thought. The Bible says, "As a man thinketh in his heart, so is he" (Proverbs 23:7). In that context we begin to get the picture — man is, or can be, in reality, that which his thoughts make him.

### Pointers
→ 1. *Be careful, some dreams do come true.*
→ 2. *Make the dream real — document it.*
→ 3. *Guide your dream time.*

### Dream believing
If you take your dream time seriously, your dream time will respond seriously. It is no good trying to bridge your integrity gap with pseudo-rationale. Belief is an active word inviting commitment. To activate your imagination and your ideas without giving them the credibility of belief is like starting any project without the confidence of success. Would you employ an executive if that executive had no belief in your marketing plan? *If you cannot believe your dreams then you should consider smaller dreams or bigger commitments*! To dream and believe requires a certain amount of faith and in that area a Christian should be prominent, because as a Christian you would accept the sovereignty of the God who made us, gave us the capacity to believe and have faith. You will notice that all people have that capacity. It is not exclusive to Christians or any other group. It is a natural component built into man. Many have been the times I have heard the wail from an individual that they had an idea or a dream a while ago but were not sure it would

work, so did nothing about it. At this point let us emphasise the dream journey procedure from a few pages ago. Clarify the dream and "walk through" the project. Your subconscious mind accepts a sleeping dream without question. Believing your *waking* dream takes it out of the world of fantasy and puts arms and legs on it. You take action. The idea is to increase your belief by following through those ideas prompted by small dreams. This in turn will establish your belief system through proven results.

### Pointers
→ 1. *Belief is credibility.*
→ 2. *Believing exposes your dreams to scrutiny.*
→ 3. *Believe small, commit small; believe big, commit big.*

### Dream big and for a purpose
The reason I suggest big dreams is because I recognise the immeasurable ability in all people. It is something of a revelation to note that no-one has ever put accurate limits on a human being, neither intellectually nor physically. All records are established to be broken; all ideas can be bettered. In discussions I have had with great achievers, I have been told time and again that each one could have gone further. They maintain they could have stretched and expanded and they believe boundaries do not exist.

Write this down, it is one of life's truisms: *the distance we can travel intellectually is directly related to the size of our dreams and the belief we have in them*! Dream big, and grow, to help those around you grow. Dream big to inspire, improve yourself and others. Dream big to prove that initiative and our democratic way can change the course of world events.

Big dreams give purpose and big purpose promotes self esteem and dignity. There is absolutely no point in wasting a good life, full in years and bursting with promise, on little dreams. Do not limit your life and choke your capacities with small dreams. But following your dreams, turning them into reality, requires another talent, and that is purpose. Many people are still playing with their dreams ten years down the track. And I hasten to point out this is not because of lack of motivation or desire. No, it is because they have not had *purpose*. Let me explain how to determine this. (Try it out with your friends.) You are told by someone they want to be rich and famous or a great achiever in a specific area. You will be able to tell in a short while whether that special magic is there by asking a simple question. Why? You will be staggered at the number of intelligent people who stumble over that question. It has been only vaguely considered. Or maybe they answer without giving it thought.

To want something for something's sake will provide the launching pad to cutting corners, use or misuse of other people, or manipulation for reasons of selfish greed. An unprincipled nature will limit the dream and certainly sour the prize. Purpose in dreaming puts the emphasis on the reason for achieving, and that is a point that should be remembered. If we pursue a dream for self-grandeur or self-edification we will naturally exclude those we love and should help; we veto their participation in the great race. The purpose of a dream and its attainment, for a Christian specifically, must include benefit or help for others, which will uplift and demonstrate principles of faith. While dreaming and planning, the honesty factor must be totally clean and the value system reaffirmed at all levels.

During my early years in business, my son Peter brought me business propositions he thought were workable and full of opportunity. He would explain the profit with comments like, "But if we could get this price, or if we could buy a little cheaper, or this happened or that happened, then we could make a profit." My response was always the same, "Son, do not try to force a profit into anything because it will invariably force its way out again." I have found over 25 years of business, profit forced is a profit I do not want, and I want to say with all conviction that a purpose forced into a dream — however worthy — is unworthy for any dream. Clear out of your mind selfishness, greed, gain for gains' sake and any thought of manipulating others or the system, and dream a dream full of purpose, pure of intent and big in dimensions which will honour God and yourself and inspire all who participate.

## Pointers
→ 1. *Your capacity is immeasurable.*
→ 2. *Do not waste time on little dreams.*
→ 3. *Dreaming expands capacity.*
→ 4. *Clarify your purpose.*
→ 5. *Never force a purpose into a dream.*
→ 6. *Make your purpose big enough for others.*

## Dream on paper — nail down the dream
To pull a dream down from the shelves of the mind on to the workbench of reality requires a naildown of ideas and thoughts on the clean framework of the written page. And this is where the foggy, the frail and the flamboyant collapse in a heap. The dream unfulfilled is just a childish fancy. If you are the least bit serious about your dream, solidarity of documentation and clarity of examination must be worked into it. Write it in a relaxed, conversational way without judgement, embellishment or qualification. Go into detail and include any new thoughts or ideas as you write. Decide you will not show this documentation to any other soul. At the same time fight back any thoughts of how others will react, what they may say or feel about that dream which is now taking shape. As you work, allow maximum time for writing and minimum time for reason, thought or reflection as you begin to cross the boundary from fantasy to reality. Do

not read or correct the dream of your life's goals until you have exhausted all and everything you want to write.

If you find you lose the flow, for whatever reason, stop and come back to it in a few days — although there is a risk that by then you may have "reasoned out" some of the great thoughts. The second time around you may have to wait for that special mood or feeling to try again.

### Pointers
→ 1. *Get the vapour on the paper.*
→ 2. *Don't reason the dream.*
→ 3. *Don't interrupt the dream.*

## Remove the nightmare

At some time or other we all have had to face a nightmare, those unspoken fears that bubble up from the deep recesses of the mind and jolt us into a waking sweat.

Psychologists and psychiatrists have probed nightmares and come up with a variety of explanations ranging from childhood terror to something we may have eaten!

So how can we remove the nightmares from our dreams and reach life's goals? Firstly, remember it is the areas of doubt within the dream that are creating the nightmare; the fear, the uncertainty. Examine now the dream you have committed to paper and add reality and reason in the areas of doubt. Bear in mind you have to come to grips with the areas in your dream that present uncertainty. For example, if you are going to be involved in high finance, but know nothing about money, you must learn the basics of high finance. If you require high levels of persuasion, then you must learn to sell, or develop the ability to select and obtain loyalty from others who will work with you. The thing to watch for is cheap advice or experience that in the long run becomes expensive. Also from expensive advice you may not get the expected return for the outlay. Do not cut corners and do not accept bad advice. Easy to say, maybe. So let us now simplify our selection process.

An example I am acquainted with is real estate. So if you are going to invest in real estate who do you go to? The property owner? Naturally not, he has a vested interest. The bank manager? No, because he has disqualified himself by being under bank supervision and if he understood investment he would be in it himself. An accountant? No. Accountants keep the score; they don't kick the goals. An investment adviser? This could be the person, but check it out carefully. A successful business-man? Yes — but put your cash on the table and pay for his advice if necessary. It may be the best advice you will get.

In the long run, the best person to seek advice from is yourself. Through careful thought and sifting and sorting through all the data, weigh up the pluses and minuses. *The final decision is yours and the results — good or bad — are yours to enjoy, or endure.* But make a decision by choice and not by circumstance. Don't expect all of the questions to be answered as there will be some that will never apply. To procrastinate is to stagnate. Remember that guarantees are not available in dreams.

The hunch, or the "gut feeling," rarely over-rides or changes facts, but its presence is not to be ignored because it can be a confirmation you are on the right track. If you make a decision, you are immediately on the move towards your life goals. If you have cleared the debris by clarifying areas of doubt and confirming areas of action then you are polishing your dream.

## Pointers
→ 1. *Test your dream for problem areas.*
→ 2. *Nightmares are problems unresolved and they need to be removed.*
→ 3. *Check the source of advice as well as the advice.*
→ 4. *Remember a good hunch or "gut-feeling" must be taken into consideration.*

### Three days of paper dreams

Many years ago, when I was desperate to understand the principles of goal-setting and I could not find anyone or any book to help me, I devised this plan to get my life together. I would recommend it only to the very desperate who cannot cope any other way. It is exhausting, time consuming, and more than a little different. Anyway it was what I needed at the time, and it solidified my life for the next ten years.

Find a place without a phone, a television set, visitors, newspapers, radios or people. Take with you sufficient food and other requirements for at least three days. Add to that a quantity of large white plain paper and pens. *On day number one* accept in your imagination that you and the world are ten years older. Draw at random, homes, automobiles, fashions and anything else that comes to your mind and how they may be ten years from now. Include matters of politics, world events, science, travel, economics and all manner of things that come into your mind. Think intently about your own physical, mental and spiritual well-being on the basis that you are ten years older. Do not divert from that path of thought and concentrate! Concentrate! Concentrate!

By the time you go to bed tired that night, you should have some impression in your conscious and unconscious thinking that the immediate worries you had are passed, your early limitations have been breeched, and the world and you have moved ahead and you are successful. This mental experience needs to be your last thought before you go to sleep ready for the morning and phase two.

*The next day*, having accepted that you are ten years older, your thoughts go to your imaginary achievements for the past ten years. Write down where you went and what you did and how you overcame all difficulties. Detail how you developed your goals, what pinnacles you reached and what rewards were yours. Also how did those around you benefit? Write down in some detail how you feel with that kind of accomplishment under your belt, and do it with conviction and embellishment. Let your mind soar as you write. Then have a restful night enjoying the exhilaration of the dream achievement.

*On day three*, you are back to reality and square one, or are you? My guess is that you will experience what I experienced and never be quite the same again. Your boundaries have been enlarged and you are ready for the challenge of reality. Now set your next ten years' goals on the basis of your previous two days' experience with the optimism of having role-played the scene and having been through it before. Do not minimise the importance or significance of such an experience nor play down the enormity of the task ahead, but use its dynamics to thrust you towards attaining your dream. In my own life, I used these principles and I exceeded my goals in my ten year plan beyond what I imagined, let alone what I had written down. I believe your response will be in direct proportion to the serious way you apply yourself to its truths.

### Pointers
→ 1. *Imagine you are ten years older.*
→ 2. *Imagine what you achieved in ten years.*
→ 3. *Write your ten year goals on the basis of experience.*

## Put life into your dreams
To put life into your dreams you must first break out of the dream cocoon. The dream cocoon has all of the comforts of the dream, but none of its obligations. It is in the cocoon, devoid of exercise and air, that most dreams stay and die. Your dream must be more than a vision confined in a cage of thought. It must, if it is to be realised, force the door of the cage and demand the challenge only found in the real world. If it dies in its delivery or on the workbench, then it either has to be put back to incubate or allowed to crumble.

Some dreams do need more incubation than others, and other dreams need more sustenance and care in the infancy stages because they are sick with problems. You have read in the previous chapters that a dream must have the permanence of paper and with that comes the opportunity to give it life and exposure to justify its existence.

Now is the time for you to make it part of your every moment by affirming continually and relentlessly its existence, its purpose and its destination. As you become involved with the mundane habits of life that beset us all, the dream must be lived in that context and in all of those moments. Your thoughts each new day must involve your regular thinking about your dream. The life that you put into your dream by affirmation and enthusiasm will eventually capture you in its net. It will be noticed by others who are close to you and very soon you will discover they are talking about it with you and with others, because of the attraction and inspiration you give the dream by the very breath you breathe into it. Your dream or goal can only exist while you give it life.

Your daily, weekly, monthly and yearly association with your dream will produce enormous returns if you keep feeding it with your enthusiasm, action and love. But it must have your commitment and closeness to develop its triumphant spirit and at times you may have to coax it forward to victory. Be prepared to nurse it when it seems frail, to activate it when it seems lazy, and to boost it even further when it is in progress. Never leave it alone for any length of time without paying attention to its requirements. Without you it is feeble and frail and could, if neglected, slip into oblivion only to be taken up by someone else who is prepared to carry it through.

Many years down the road you may come across a piece of paper written many years earlier about a dream that could have been a magnificent obsession, lost through the sluice gates of apathy, neglect or indifference.

Yet your dream belongs only to you and is only achievable while you give it life. In giving it life, you have ensured its destiny.

### Pointers
→ 1. *Break out of the dream cocoon.*
→ 2. *Only you can give your dream life.*
→ 3. *Live the dream to its ultimate destiny.*

## Plan and work the dream

The planning of your goals should be exciting because you are dealing with your own destiny, exercising the awesome power of choice and documenting the timing and process of action. Planning is a means. The means may change from time to time, but you will never change the ultimate goals which is your life plan. Nevertheless, planning is important.

This process of planning must assess and evaluate all aspects of your strategy and document in detail the track you need to run on. The direction that will be taken together with the provisions of knowledge, people, location and timing, all relate to the ultimate destination. At first *particular attention should be paid to timing*. Every goal has a time frame to which everything else must conform. To have a goal without clarity of timing, is to move back into the zone of wishful thinking and away from objective and determined planning. Spend prime time evaluating carefully what is your ultimate date for reaching your goal, carefully considering all aspects including your age, the projected economic and political climate and social trends.

*Next, deal with supportive goals*, such as capital, mental and logistical requirements in relation to a time frame. Take into consideration the run-up factors of acquiring these needs to fit in with your life goals.

Suddenly your goals take form. You have the supportive building blocks to reach the summit. Do a countdown in all areas including minor goals and supportive requirements to reach them. Draw up timetables and achievement levels which must be reached before progressing further.

This planning your goals, step by step, time partition by time partition, providing a working chart will ultimately allow you to revise and revaluate, because it now has time and form which can be objectively analysed.

**Pointers**
→ 1. *Planning gives form to your dreams.*
→ 2. *Timetables and time frames provide the structure for completion.*
→ 3. *Do a countdown in all areas to complete the plans.*

The plan is now in its elementary form and it must be put to the test in the real world. At this point the shine and the glow lose some of their lustre as hard reality sets in. Whatever you do, do not change the plan just because you receive some hard knocks, disappointments or setbacks, because it is at this point the dream is confirmed. No dream in reality goes as easily as the visionary dream. That is why we have spent so much time in previous chapters, clarifying, sorting and confirming. It is at this point you realise just how much of a nightmare and the illusion you have removed.

*Working your dream becomes a real test of your endurance, patience and faith.* It weeds out the casual and the theoretical philosopher from the pragmatic worker who is expecting, willing and anxious to pay the price and endure the pain. At this time again your value system will be tested and your pain endurance proved for the climb to the summit. Working the dream means using every effort within your capabilities to put in the time and effort and make it succeed.

There is a big difference between activity and

productivity. Many salesmen today think all they have to do is to make enough presentations of goods to customers and they will succeed. Not so. You must go to as many customers as can buy and tell them the right things, that's the way to succeed. Hard work alone will not win the day. Working your dream until you drop may not achieve anything unless you prepare yourself in whatever way necessary to complete the job.

The first essential is to work on yourself relentlessly. I knew a man who had a huge goal. He spent thirty days with every book he could find on the subject. He passed hours on the phone chasing up every single item on which he needed more information. He worked the plan by realising he himself was the biggest component part of it. The thirty days he spent alone in the early days pushed him light years ahead of others who attempted to do what he has achieved. So, with the early skills in order, attack your minor goals and deadlines with enthusiasm, knowing the action starts and ends with you! Like a moon rocket which uses most of the fuel at the commencement, and then requires less energy after it passes the earth's gravitational pull, you will find that getting launched is the hardest part.

In my case, I did not prepare myself completely in the early years, so I had to suffer the discomfort of going broke three times to learn the lessons. In learning, I was able to develop a more reliable tool myself to get the job done. You may have some false starts and setbacks, but to the sincere goal achiever and dream-maker these are only temporary. After many years on the road they fade as minor irritations one had to endure.

Never allow yourself to make excuses, like thinking you are "too honest to succeed." In working your plan you will find yourself looking for excuses or scapegoats when things start to go wrong. If you look anywhere else but to yourself and your plans you are doomed to failure.

**Pointers**
→ 1. *You are the first thing to work on.*
→ 2. *Don't confuse false starts and delays with failure.*
→ 3. *Never seek to make excuses — look to find and solve the problem.*

### Expand the dream

One of the continued surprises of my life is that goals and dreams continue to expand. You will open up one avenue of endeavour only to find another opening as well. And the more that you find to do, the more there is to do. Usually more exciting and interesting than before. As you start to work your dream by first working on yourself, you will discover you have other abilities, and the process, it seems, goes on throughout life. Opportunities continue coming forward offering further incentive and challenge to meet your life goals.

*The chance of you attaining your life dreams are good; the chances of exceeding them are overwhelming.* You will be compelled time and time again to ask yourself the questions, "Why didn't I think of it before?" and "Can I expect much more?" The answer to the latter is yes, because you are no longer indecisive, hesitant, and without clear purpose. You are now on a firm track, running toward a predetermined destination, which you have chosen.

Under this kind of posture you cannot help but discover changes in your personality and character, developing attitudes and interests in different directions. Any expansion of your dream must take as its pivot point your ultimate goals and must not veer from your course, however tempting or fanciful it may seem at the time. I have seen many goals and dreams shattered by distraction or diversion of interest under all kinds of good and even benevolent disguises, only to find the recipient will move off the tracks and be a long way off course before the bitterness of distraction is felt. You move away from your ultimate goal at your peril. However, some changes may be made after careful examination to enhance and speed up the process.

Make sure any changes are tested and proven, usefully and successfully, before commitment. Expand your goal carefully and avoid doing it while you are under stress or on the crest of a wave. During such times your emotions can be on full throttle, and emotion in any person has a bad history in relation to integrity.

**Pointers**
→ 1. *As you grow, your dream will grow.*
→ 2. *Allow your dream to expand.*
→ 3. *Don't change direction without inspection.*

In fact, early disappointment can be very helpful by alerting you to an unrecognised problem, preventing a huge catastrophe further down the track. So treat it as a friend, acknowledging its reality, examining its credentials and impact as an act of preventive medicine for the future.

Resurrect whatever you can from your disappointment as there are always bits and pieces that can be put back into the mainstream of your dream. If you look at it carefully with a positive attitude, and if you use creative imagination, you may even find a way to turn the problem into a propeller. You need to reach your next level.

**Pointers**
→ 1. *Disappointments are inevitable.*
→ 2. *Your dream is stronger than your disappointment.*
→ 3. *Early disappointment can help you.*

**Lean on your dream**
To lean on a dream at times of frustration seems to be

the only thing left to do. You know your dream can hold the weight and so the best thing is to hold on and wait.

We need to lean on our dreams and use our ingenuity to create ideas and opportunities. Stoppages or blockages at any time create frustration, particularly when our planning is right and we have done everything we can about the situation. At these times we must concentrate our minds on our dream and our ultimate objective and ask the question, "What can I do during this frustrating delay that will act as a catalyst to either remove the object of the frustration, or make use of the frustration and obtain a benefit?"

# Disappointments, Frustration and Failure

# CHAPTER SIX

# Disappointments, Frustration And Failure

## Frustration and creativity

I remember once being delayed at an international airport; fogged in with nowhere to go. I sat down and started to think about my life and my behaviour. I asked myself a series of questions, enquiring as it were, why I did or did not do certain things. It was a worthy time of self analysis and some of the answers I have been able to pass on to many others with some benefit.

Another time I recall the way I worked my way out of a seemingly frustrating disappointment with humour and resolve. It was when my car's automatic transmission broke down and I simply could not afford the repair bill. I was thousands of miles from my destination and I had to get there to keep my business going. The mechanic laid all the pieces out on the cement floor and said, "The whole transmission is worn out and needs completely replacing." When he quoted the figure I went into orbit. I could not pay it and I was in deep despair.

Then I did a remarkable thing. I leaned on my dream and resolved to get this car fixed and hit the road. I reasoned it would be impossible for every part of my transmission to be totally worn out. I knew zero about cars. So I figured I would speak to the mechanic in ignorance — with a dash of humour — and check out the answer to some questions. I examined each part of the transmission with the mechanic following me. I asked him could he weld this? Expand that? File this? Replace that and pack it with washers? Tighten this? Put springs on that? Get a secondhand piece to put in? I reached the point where the mechanic was in fits of laughter, and in a good-humoured way, he came to the party with the alternative suggestions and alterations. The end result was I got back into my car for a fraction of the cost and reached my destination. (Incidentally, I sold that car with another 60,000 miles on the clock and the transmission was as strong as ever!)

Believe frustration and seeming failure can be a time of creativity and learning.

## Disappointment as challenge

Disappointments are the testing times. They provide opportunities to evaluate your resolves and test your determination quotient before the next step. During times of disappointment your attitude is of paramount importance because it is at that level your enthusiasm can be accelerated or deflated.

The handling of your first disappointment should be accepted as a direct challenge to your ultimate goal and your personal management ability. Evaluate its occurrence and results as you would if you were a probing scientist.

### Pointers
→ 1. *Frustration can be time-creating.*
→ 2. *Frustration can be a time of reassessment.*
→ 3. *Frustration can force us to develop our persistence and perceptive powers.*

## Failure is temporary

Failure all too often brings with it the incriminating accusation of worthlessness. It can be fiendishly judgemental or devastatingly humiliating and it sows the seeds of doubt.

It is true, success tends to smooth the memory of doubt and failure. Conversely, failure brings the feeling of worthlessness.

At one time when I failed I had nothing but a mountain of debts — equivalent to five years salary for a top executive. I also had no job and no opportunity with which to attack the problem. But I had a dream that was still real and vivid in my mind, and though I was utterly exhausted, I used that dream to get on my feet, grease the wheels and affirm life's goals with God's call and hand upon my life. During those difficult months with creditors, I was smiling deep down inside because I could still see the fulfilled dream, the complete picture. I handled that catastrophe by putting it into its limited time frame and leaning on my dream.

Any failure is only a temporary setback that will appear from the most unlikely of places and through the most unlikely of circumstances, but the stronger you cling to that dream the easier it is to push through.

*Remember, you are only a permanent failure when you have decided to give up.*

### Pointers
→ 1. *Dreams can act as protective barriers against failure.*
→ 2. *Failure is only a temporary condition.*
→ 3. *Failure can be a step up.*

## Reassessment

There will come a time of reassessment and reflection when you will ask yourself the question, "Is it all worth it and am I on the right track?" The important point to remember here is you are still talking about means, not about your final destination. Rarely will the life goal come into question. The real question is: "*Will I reach my goal*, and am I on the right track?"

Times of reassessment can be good because they force you again to evaluate your progress and the methods you are applying to reach your goal. *Now is the time to reaffirm your ultimate dream and relive it*. The focus must always be on the life goal.

In your assessment, be factual about accomplishments so far, and if they are minimal, examine the reasons why in detail. Pay particular attention to your own performance (you may like to read my book *How To Be Happy Though Rich* to get some more help). Small achievements cannot be measured on their immediate returns but rather on the lessons learned and the effect they had, and will have, upon you. Examine your time frames and see if they need some readjustment. Look for obsolete items that are no longer applicable to the overall goal. Seek to streamline the process and look for legitimate shortcuts that will allow you to catch up on your timetable without imparing the whole programme. Also search for innovations or methods recently discovered which could make your existing path obsolete, or new machinery that could save time or give you more information. Find out if you can develop a new method of financing to enable you to take a quantum jump without putting yourself at risk. New and faster methods can be adopted to do all kinds of things over the coming years, and when they appear, you may say, "Why didn't I think of that?"

Use your fantastic ability to think and test new ideas by role-playing them in your mind. If successful, you will find you have used your time of reassessment to thrust forward rather than to sink into a rut. Take this important period of your life to uphold your dream and iron out problem areas. Areas of doubt should be dealt with and attacked with positive vigour. Do not put off or ignore the reassessment, but rather greet the opportunity with positive expectancy.

It takes a certain amount of courage to face a reassessment so in that respect it should be welcomed as a true friend.

## Pointers

→ 1. *Reassessment can be very helpful.*
→ 2. *Reassessment can strengthen your resolve.*
→ 3. *Reassessment is reaffirming.*

CHAPTER SEVEN

# Why Goals For Life?

# CHAPTER SEVEN

# **Why Goals For Life?**

### Life and time

All of us have been given the gift called life, although some have it longer than others. Many of us measure life by its duration and hope and pray for longevity with health to enjoy its benefits. Some may look back on their life's journey with regret and disappointment, while others see it as a bland series of events moving towards an uneventful end. *Life must be measured in something more meaningful than time.* Surely life is more than that.

Some people come and go in a short lifetime, but manage to leave an indelible mark on history which affects the lives of generations to come. Jesus Christ changed the course of history and yet His earthly time with us was limited to thirty-three years. The time frame you have been given here on earth has not been revealed to you. But putting aside accidental death, life is continually being extended by medical science and seventy years is now the average limit.

But even our doctors can be wrong in assessing termination of life under what they consider clear and predictable circumstances.

Many years ago my wife and I were called to the doctor's surgery and were told that my wife's mother could not hope to live out the year as her heart was in such a bad condition. She lived on another ten years and contributed greatly to others around her. I believe the extension was in relationship to her dreams.

You have been given your life, whatever its time frame, to use wisely and well. Not in subjective form but in objective form to achieve and to grow for your benefit and the benefit of others. To trade that opportunity for a limited goal over a limited time frame, and not to use it for its full measure, is in effect rejecting its usefulness and its worth. Over the years I have noticed those who retire and have no further goals die or are confined to total medical care within a few short years. But those who retire in a positive way seem to slip into another gear and another role and get a new lease of life and activity in the process. They extend their lives even further.

The real high-flyers are those who have the magnificent obsession that could be expanded to a thousand years. They would strive, plan, stretch until their last breath, enjoying it to the hilt. A short life shut down in the middle of a goal still leaves behind a level of commitment reached, and something else — an inspiration for those who were fortunate enough to know and work with the person concerned. Having said all of that, life's time frame is still relatively predictable and the number reaching senior years is growing considerably every decade. So you are on the side of predictability and your chances of surviving to old age are almost guaranteed.

### Pointers
→ 1. *Life's time frame is weighted heavily on the side of longevity.*
→ 2. *Life goals give and extend life.*
→ 3. *Life must be measured in doing, not dying.*

**Second best?**

Short little spurts of energy and hesitant steps to progress along with short-term, limited goals are really second best. A goal for, say, two years, or even ten years, without a master plan for life, leaves no room for hope and no hope for room. To accept short-term assignments throughout life is to take life in little nibbles, never savouring the banquet. To have your life limited by accident or illness is one thing. To limit your own life by self-limitation is something quite different. Accident or illness takes it out of your hands, but self-limitation squashes its potential. You never realise the enormity of the opportunities before you. Cutting your life up into little pieces without a grand plan is stifling your achievement quotient. It may give variety, but it rarely gives satisfaction.

With a life goal comes variety. You could, of course, have a life goal of small goals, which would give you a series of goals and achievement timetables, but for what purpose? You see, one's purpose must be included, and then you are back on the track of setting life's goals. Then we are walking in unison with what we were created for.

Accepting second best is an admittance of perpetual failure, but the tide is so easily turned by just focusing our attention on our ultimate goal or purpose. Maybe you consider it selfish to programme your life to achieve a magnificent obsession. So why not take the focus off yourself and put it on your achievement for someone or something else?

*Taking life seriously glorifies God; taking life flippantly glorifies man.* Setting goals for life with purpose and commitment guarantees benefits and progress to all. Protecting yourself from long-term commitment and purpose is wasting life and abandoning responsibility to all mankind. All of us must, if we are to exhibit integrity, pull our fair share of the load. By opting out of goals for life, we waste our abilities and opportunities, and therefore accept second best.

Your best cannot be done by someone else! It is unique to you and only cashable by you; not to spend it means the world is the poorer. We should not measure ourselves against others by direct comparisons because we are all different. But we may see others who have not been blessed with some of our gifts and opportunities and yet who have surpassed us in their achievements.

This is when we must evaluate ourselves with — not against — others. Second best shrivels up character and says to our children, "Here is the benchmark I have set as a standard for you. Do not go beyond it — second best is best for us." Your family and friends will recognise the benchmark and you will recognise your failure and folly. Second best is not good enough — life is worth our best effort, and we need to be committed to plan for it.

### Pointers
→ 1. *Second best is putting down yourself.*
→ 2. *Second best is a bad benchmark for others.*
→ 3. *Second best is not directly a measurement.*

## Commitment level

I was driving in my car with a long-time friend but my mind was away thinking and strategising. My friend said, "Peter, you're not really here, what in the world are you thinking about?" I told him I was trying to work out how I could get more done, fit more into my life plan and achieve more than I had been achieving. My friend responded with, "How in the world do you expect to get anything more done? You already have out-stripped and out-performed everyone I know. You are already achieving more in a day than I am achieving in a week. When you talk like that you just make me feel tired."

My friend made the mistake that many people make and that is accepting that our commitment level is full. *The fact is, a commitment level is expandable and its size cannot be measured.* Commitment has no relationship to time, and therefore cannot be harnessed in a time frame. A mistake most people make on the commitment level is this: they put restraints on it that are unrelated to it and try to make it work within boundaries and laws which apply to something else. Your time commitment may be full — but I doubt it. You can always rearrange and improve it. But your commitment level has to do with something much less tangible, because commitment concerns integrity, life's personal principles and value systems.

Commitment level is often measured by business rather than progress. Being committed to a project, person or organisation must have the measure of objectivity placed against it. Against that criterion, dare I suggest that your commitment level is not full? The next question is, "Does it have to be full?" So, what is full? I do not regard it as full if it is overflowing to the point of frustration and panic; and I certainly do not consider it full if you are coasting along. I do say it is full when you honestly believe you are using your commitment level wisely and doing what you can where you can within the perimeters of life's goals and integrity. To waste a portion of your commitment level is to waste life and to waste life is wrong indeed. If you are doing things with absolute integrity, you will find your commitment level will automatically expand itself when a great opportunity or need occurs.

Commitments keep us growing and stretching and when we grow and stretch in a new direction, we enter the most rewarding and interesting areas of life.

Some years ago a young couple came to me for help in the area of planning meetings — they wanted to be first-rate convention organisers. We discussed the commitment required and they responded, yes, they thought their commitment level was already full. But they saw a need and wanted to meet that need. Together we arranged for bigger meetings than they had ever organised and in stretching to meet that commitment, they never once went back to their previous level. Their commitment boundaries were expanded. Almost every time I meet them now, I see their boundaries extended even further.

### Pointers
→ 1. *Commitment boundaries can be widened.*
→ 2. *Commitment must not be confused with time.*
→ 3. *Commitments once made guarantee growth.*

## What would you be prepared to trade your life for?

Is an unplanned life better than a planned life? Ask yourself that question and then check what principles you base your answer on. Would you jump on a Jumbo jet and zoom off around the world without planning where you were going? Would you let a brain surgeon operate on you, knowing he was just going to "feel his way through" and make up his mind as he went? Of course not! That's preposterous. But wait, it's not really, because in each case we are dealing with life, and in many instances we are prone to wander along without purpose. Without life's goals, there is no purpose.

If all we are going to do is drift along like a rudderless ship, why not trade that life in and get another — one that has purpose and dignity and will benefit others. I see that trade as a bargain, and the price is commitment. What you receive on the trade is coming alive to the possibilities of your own growth, and in so doing you help others to grow. Most importantly, you will create self worth because you are reaching out from yourself to lift the needy and disadvantaged of the world. Is that not better than self indulgence or trading off for a lower value?

*Your life is valuable, and the use to which you put it increases its value.* With inherent gifts and developed skills, it brings with it a grateful spirit directed by a loving God who cares for you and is committed to your development. He is blessed by your accomplishment.

**Pointers**
→ 1. *Life cannot accept anything less than it's equivalent.*
→ 2. *Without life goals you cheapen life's values.*
→ 3. *With life goals you realise life's worth.*

## Examples of life goals

The Bible has sharply defined principles for us to follow and secular investigation and science have never been able to weaken its authority. On the contrary, they have reinforced Biblical history with each new discovery. And it is interesting to note that God gave His chosen servants goals for life.

Abraham was given a life's goal, and it was promised, under obedience, that it would continue for generations to come.

Moses was given a life's goal to deliver the Israelites to the Promised Land; only at the point of his delivery, were his life and task finished.

Saul was made king and, although he disobeyed God, David was unable to harm him. Saul's anointing could not be removed because of the sacredness of his life goal.

David was given a life goal which he fulfilled.

Hannah had a life goal for her son, Samuel, and through God he marched through the pages of Biblical history as a prophet, demonstrating his life's call.

Joseph was given a life's goal and through ridicule, suffering and opposition, he reached it.

Add to these so many more who were given life goals by God — Sampson, John the Baptist, Peter the fisherman and Jonah — and finally, Jesus Christ, whose goal was our salvation. The abundance of goal-setters in history should be a guide and example to us all, and confirm its commission from the Almighty Father.

**Pointers**
→ 1. *God gave life goals in Biblical times.*

→ 2. *Life goals control the life.*
→ 3. *Life goals have a Biblical pattern which should apply in our lives.*

The pages of commercial history are dotted with the famous and the rich, who set a life goal achieving what many thought was impossible. In Australia we had Sir Sidney Kidman, who as a 13-year-old boy with almost no education left home in 1870 for a perilous journey through outback Australia. Only 10 years earlier the famous explorers Burke and Wills had perished in the same area. Kidman came from a large family and had worked in the cattle yards since he was 10. Now, with a one-eyed aged mare he purchased called "Cyclops," and a half a dollar in savings, he set out to learn the cattle business on the big cattle farms of Australia. Sidney had a dream which was to focus itself into a life goal to breed and market cattle in the cheap, unpredictable, wild areas of Australia. His plan was to establish a string of properties stretching from the north to the south of Australia, following the waterways. This would keep the new colony fed, and expand export markets around the world. Sidney Kidman became the biggest property owner in the British Empire, and without a doubt the single largest cattle owner in the world at that time. He was affectionately known as "the cattle king." Young Sidney reached his life goals.

W. Clement Stone as a young boy lived without a father, but was blessed with a remarkable mother. From his humble beginnings, by choice and by planned life goals, he became the most respected and the most wealthy life assurance man in the world today. I have asked him many times about those early years and he speaks with confidence and enthusiasm of reaching his life goals. Today he is known as Mr. P.M.A. (Mr. Positive Mental Attitude). Ten minutes in the presence of W. Clement Stone can change your life. He deliberately set his life goals and he reached them (as this goes to print he will be 83 years of age and still working).

The late Ray Kroc was a paper cup salesman. At 54 years of age he developed a magnificent obsession to buy a hamburger franchise from two brothers called McDonald. Today he has one of the largest takeaway food franchises in the world. Ray Kroc didn't start his life goals until he was 54, but within 26 years he reaped a gross annual turnover of one billion dollars. He also is attributed with having made more millionaires than anyone else over these last three decades.

The world of business abounds with stories of real life situations where life goals have catapulted ordinary people, with seemingly limited experience and ability, into giants of stature and achievement. Paul J. Meyer of Success Motivation Institute in Texas is probably the world authority on goal-setting. He has documented stories that make you sit on the edge of your seat with excitement as he unfolds one case history after another of life's goal-setters who have achieved and are still achieving the seemingly impossible. Super business achievers are life goal-setters. They have no limitations on their dreams, and will not tolerate the disturbance or the distraction of little dreams or occasional goals. High achievers plan long and keep short accounts with their own ability, measuring it, coaxing it, upgrading it and progressing it to fit into the context of those life goals.

## Pointers
→ 1. *Big commercial achievers set life goals.*
→ 2. *Life goals can start at any time.*
→ 3. *Life goals are definitely for life.*

Explorers have a remarkable track record towards life goal commitments, infused as those goals may be with danger, discomfort and disability. From Christopher Columbus to navigator James Cook — who "left nothing unattempted," as it was said — they come in all sizes, shapes and colours.

Goal-setters today find themselves in space shuttles or probing the deepest oceans. You must occasionally ask yourself, "What is it that pushes them on — fame, fortune or immortality?" I think not, because many receive little recognition or remuneration for their efforts. That strange force that propels man towards life goals crosses cultural and international barriers confirming that such goals are for the entire human race, both demanded and required.

### Pointers
→ 1. *Life goals are often accepted without reward or recognition.*
→ 2. *Life goals for mankind are trans-national.*
→ 3. *Life goals have been with us since the very beginning of recorded history.*

### Satisfaction creates motivation

It is a helpless position to be in, wanting to achieve but having nothing worth achieving. *The absence of a goal is probably one of the most destructive forces facing some people.* To commit your life to something worthwhile will give you the motivation and the energy you need to get the job done. Motivation does not come from "nowhere" to go "somewhere" — it must come from something specific to go somewhere specific. That drifting feeling comes from lack of deadlines and absence of pressure to meet a timetable through a fulfilled commitment.

I hope that reading this book will give you the inspiration towards motivation. But it will never give you motivation. To want motivation is to invite pressure and commitment. On a hot, humid summer's day out in the country you do not feel under any compulsion to run or expend any energy, but the sudden appearance of a poisonous snake at your feet propels you into the championship league of the short sprint. You are the same person, in the same place, with the same thoughts, until suddenly you are motivated, compelling you to take action, and action you take!

Life needs pressure. The essence of being motivated is knowing where you are going and knowing you are on the right track with a compelling desire to get there. The beauty of goal-setting is that its creative force is exclusively personal.

This not only produces satisfaction from knowing where you are going, but it also produces satisfaction by increasing your own self-esteem and in so doing it creates a self-love that inspires. In my experience motivation has only been sustained by an individual who has written life goals with deadlines and measurements, all put together in a parcel an individual believes in.

The most motivated man I have ever met is Dr. John Edmund Haggai, who was so sickly as a child he was not expected to survive. Yet today, at over sixty, he is one of the finest human physical specimens I know. It has been said by many, "Spend ten minutes on the phone with John Haggai and you feel you can conquer the world." John Haggai produces continually, and relentlessly, and persistently, all with good humour. He exudes integrity and has an obvious love for those around him. But John Haggai has a dream, and through the Haggai Institute of Advanced Leadership Training in Singapore, he is rewriting the missionary programme and the spiritual history books of Christendom for the whole third world.

John has a life goal on paper, with deadlines and a dedicated commitment. How can you stop a man like that? But more importantly, look at how you can start a man like that.

Life goals are the answer to satisfaction.

**Pointers**
→ 1. *Satisfaction is knowing where you are going.*

→ 2. *Satisfaction creates motivation and motivation increases satisfaction.*

→ 3. *Motivation means pressure and commitment.*

## Personal goals

Have you ever had a great thought, idea or dream about a particular course of action in which you would like to engage? Have you felt the excitement rise as the dream becomes more clear and the programme seems more realistic? You then meditate upon that thought, idea or dream a little more, and realise how great it is and how it can be achieved. You then decide to tell your spouse or friend about it. But as you reveal it with all the excitement of a six-year-old child, you are faced with a blank stare and a well-mannered, "Isn't that nice for you?" response. Why is it so difficult to transfer a dream to someone else?

The reason is that *a dream is personal.* It is personal because it reflects the sum total of your environmental and imaginative experience, and cannot reflect or produce the experiences of another individual. Goals, too, are deeply personal, but have the added power of emphasis. Goals are the next step to realism. In one giant leap they take you from the unreal to the real, still retaining the exclusivity of the dream. And the possibilities of your dream, because of its personal nature, may never be attempted by someone else; it cannot be duplicated by another.

Do not treat your dreams as if they were community property, but as your very own to protect and cherish and bring to reality.

### Pointers

→ 1. *Dreams have the privacy of the individual.*

→ 2. *Dreams, like goals, have the validity of belonging.*

→ 3. *Do not treat your dreams as community property.*

## Energy

You know those annoying situations. There you are fatigued and flat, feeling like a wrung-out dishcloth. Then, boom, someone bursts in full of energy and throbbing with action. The energy quotient of some individuals can leave you gasping, just as the lack of it in others can leave you feeling annoyed. Energy is not as predictable as you may think. A youngster on a school day morning can resemble a snail in reverse gear. But on Saturday morning he is powered on rocket fuel as he dives out of bed, gets dressed in record time and is waiting by the car, football in hand, urging on his half-dressed father.

The remarkable degree of energy available to do what we want to do, would like to do — or by fear are forced to do — gives us some hint of its redeemability. *The energy level does not question the need, but it responds to your mental condition and motivation.*

There was a time when I considered myself only mildly fit when some cattle I had bought broke through a fence and strolled into rough country where I had to give chase on foot. I was desperate to get them back, knowing that if they reached a deep gorge I would lose them for keeps. I finally got the stock out, and I returned to the farmhouse exhausted, with my clothes in tatters. When I eventually figured out how far I had run I estimated I had covered some five miles in heavy clothes over some of the most difficult and steep terrain in the district. If I had been challenged to compete over that sort of country I would have thought it impossible. But, with purpose and strong motivation, I did it.

Energy is personal and can be produced at will in certain circumstances. As you become more experienced at it you will find you can produce enormous amounts of energy — if the correct circumstances are present. *Your energy thrust, or lack of it, is in direct proportion to your most desired or feared task.* In this context, your life goals can be reached by combining your great dreams with action to ignite that energy force.

Also remember, your energy level cannot be directly transferred to others, but your enthusiasm and inspiration can help trigger energy in others. Use energy wisely, direct it carefully and acknowledge its usefulness.

**Pointers**

→ 1. *Energy can be expanded, but only for you.*
→ 2. *Energy commitment is your choice.*
→ 3. *Energy can serve well your life goals.*


**Pain**

Some years ago, I was in hospital in great pain. The doctors were working on me and I was grunting and groaning with perspiration pouring out of me. I noticed through a gap in the curtain the man in the bed next to me sipping his coffee and reading a book. I wanted to scream out, "Don't you know what I'm going through?" But I knew he couldn't and there was no way I could transfer the pain to him! Yes, well we know it, pain is personal.

When I lost everything and went broke many years ago, I experienced pain which stayed with me in varying degrees for months. My friends could not relate to my suffering. Years later a friend lost everything in a particular deal and I phoned long distance to speak with him about the pain he was going through. He said, "You are the first person I've spoken to who understands."

"That's because I once felt it," I replied.

Pain in its isolation indicates our personal responsibility for our own lives and the individual acceptance of our own suffering. The suffering is a deeply personal experience and the pain endurance (mentioned in a previous chapter of this book) forms a bond between the personal aspects of goal-setting and the personal aspects of pain.

Just as it is impossible to transfer pain, it is also impossible to transfer your life goals to someone else, expecting them to feel or endure the pain that comes with their achievements. Certainly pain can be reduced or removed by medication, but in its removal comes a danger of not respecting it — and doing more damage.

Link your life goals to pain. They are personal, felt only by you, not transferable and only avoidable by deadening the relevant area. Goals demand pain. Some years ago, during a particularly difficult time in business, I wished I could just go to sleep and wake up twelve months down the road when the difficulties had blown over. Alas, that was not to be and by experiencing the difficulties — and personally feeling the pain — I am much wiser.

Pain is a warning, a teacher, a protector and can be the personal catalyst to reach our life goals.

### Pointers
→ 1. *Pain is always personal.*
→ 2. *Pain can only be understood by those who have endured it.*
→ 3. *Pain can be a personal catalyst.*

### Loneliness
From time to time things will go wrong and, to put it bluntly, you will feel rotten. The depth of your feelings will be directly related to the foolishness or lack of attention to detail that brought about the misery. From an outsider's point of view you may have seen someone who is suffering and wondered why they got so uptight about mistakes in life. The point is, quite often we blow our mistakes out of proportion, which hurts us more and makes recovery slower. Mistakes, failures and errors of judgement are going to happen from time to time, and we will feel alone. Feeling alone will occur whether we are supported by others or not.

*Loneliness is a natural component of life experienced by all who are determined to make something of their lives.* It is not that we disregard the preferred comfort of friends and family. These are always significant assets to us all, and the special bond and affection of a close family is the best support anyone can have. But even with the strongest family or friendship support, the bottom line always exposes itself: It all really depends on me and I had better get back to the bench quickly, do some repair work and push on. To wallow in the comfort of friends and family is to slip back further into failure and despair. Very often what we need is a kick in the pants to increase our fighting spirit, rather than a soft shoulder to cry on.

Don't get me wrong — I know we need comfort and support from those we love, but that is to be a temporary thing to dress the wounds and comfort the patient. After a while (and the shorter the time the better), we go back into the battle, bandages, wounds and all, and fight on towards our life goal.

Loneliness in life goals is natural because these goals are yours alone, and you must accept the full responsibility for the results or lack of results. The danger is to think that you can do it all alone, without support and encouragement. Without family and friends you must do the next best thing — encourage yourself. And how do you do that? By affirmation, auto-suggestion, reading good inspirational material (such as biographies) — and of course, prayer.

When the axe does fall, you must take the blow yourself, and take full responsibility. During these times you feel what thousands have felt before you, that is the loneliness of leadership. For example, if you are in business and something does go wrong can you tell your bank manager? Of course not! He may well cut off financial supply. Can you share it with your staff? No, because they are looking to you for solutions, motivation and security. Well, can you share it with a competitor? Wrong again. He will be happy to know and take advantage of the set-back. Can you tell your spouse? Well, I am sure that if I told my wife, it would double the trouble because she would start worrying about me. So let's face it. When things go wrong, loneliness will be a natural component. But for the Christian it creates a strong vertical relationship in prayer with God Himself.

**Pointers**
→ 1. *Accept loneliness as a natural component of life.*
→ 2. *Accept the comfort of family and friends as a breathing space only.*
→ 3. *Nobody is going to fix the problem but you, so push on.*


Of course, when things go right, share the glory and excitement with your family, friends and helpers. At times of victory it is only right you encourage as much participation as possible. Make the victories in your life goals special occasions because nobody will work faithfully and competently forever without some recognition. While you are at this point take a back seat, even if you are at the centre of attention. Too much involvement in the adoration of the crowd will separate you from your energy and next objective. Relish your victory when you are completely alone, knowing full well you set a goal and achieved it. Victory, like pain and loss, is a personal matter, and no one else can ever quite feel like a victor.

A point worth mentioning here is that people of high achievement are often accused of being aloof and independent, but I do not believe that is a fair generalisation. Such an attitude shown by goal-setters and achievers is an expression of their dedication and commitment to a predetermined goal and not a reflection against other people. On the victory "high," also guard against making any dramatic shift in your life's goal plan. Wait for a sober moment to reassess if you feel it necessary.

**Pointers**
→ 1. *Even in success you can be alone.*
→ 2. *Separating yourself from others because of your strong commitment is automatic.*
→ 3. *Do not change plans when you are on a victory "high."*

# How To Find Goals

# CHAPTER EIGHT

# How To Find Goals

## Your story

There are many ways to find your own life goals and many people already know them, but they have not taken the trouble to verbalise them or put them on to paper for examination. Throughout this book I have tried to get you acquainted with writing to crystalise your thinking and give your goals form and substance. The method I am about to suggest is another one I have found helpful, and it may be a valuable tool to clarify your own goals.

In previous chapters I have discussed dreaming, visualising and imagining as a means of creating and solidifying goals. Now I am going to delve deeper as I think it will give some extra clarity.

Think of yourself as being 90 years of age. You have to write your life story. *What will your main theme be*? Is there a particular force in your life that keeps appearing and progressing toward the ultimate, achievable and measurable goal? How will you start your biography after you get through the incidentals of birth, school and other events?

Does a particular thought or objective gnaw at the very

root of your life, pestering it and pulling at it, demanding attention for its fulfilment? Can you weave something of a plot through the mystery of your life that has its fulfilment in the recovery of something lost, or the creating of something new or the protection of something good?

Is it possible to get into the story something of perspective and circumstance that makes your heart skip a beat or builds up in you an ache that finally gives way to a sigh of relief on its discovery?

What will your main theme really be? *Is there anything that you would particularly emphasise that would show you in a better light?* How far would you be prepared to embellish that emphasis? What would you be seeking to play down in this biography that you would prefer not to mention or expand upon? How would you describe your habits, morals and relationships with others?

Why not write it down again, not as you see it now, but as you would like it to be? See the difference you put on the emphasis and circumstance. Now you are starting to face up to your life goals.

### Pointers
→ 1. *Imagine you are 90 and writing your life story.*
→ 2. *What would your main theme be?*
→ 3. *What would you play down and what would you embellish?*
→ 4. *Use this experiment to clarify your life goals.*

### Emotion
If you knew for a certainty you could achieve your heart's desire, how would you react? Would you be satisfied in keeping it as it is, or would you — knowing of its certainty — lose interest and want something extremely different?

Your heart's desire should be examined for emotional stability, with the froth and bubble of sense and feeling removed, to expose the integrity and substance of its existence. Not that I am devoid of or against emotion per se, but I am wary of emotion unless I can see the substance of surety or the evidence of fact. Let me illustrate. I love my family and the evidence is the way I care for them and protect them. The emotional side of my affection is consistent with the evidence of my behaviour, and the fact of my consistent support. With our heart's desires we should express more than just emotional commitment if we want to achieve tangible results. No-one else can commit you to your heart's desire because it has the singular emphasis of your life upon it and, although in some respects others may have similar desires, the attainment of those desires affects all differently.

Desires are sometimes wishful thinking, usually in the realm of the impossible or the improbable. If we could get our desires, I often wonder how long we would be satisfied. I have known people to have a desire for money, only to find that on attaining it they still do not feel fulfilled. It seems the only form of fulfilment in the realm of money and material possessions is to have just a little bit more.

But if you really want to achieve your heart's desire why not set that as a goals programme with time frames and points for evaluation? Assess its affect upon you and calculate its purpose in relation to yourself and others. Visualise it, energise it, dream it and give it the permanence of paper.

Some people just don't seem to take these matters seriously, but the clear evidence is *if you don't plan something today you won't gain something tomorrow*, because we are either today what circumstances have made us or what we have made of circumstances.

## Pointers
→ 1. *Examine the emotion in your desire and make sure it has integrity.*
→ 2. *Clarify your heart's desire against the guarantee*

*of its attainment.*
→ 3. *Qualify your heart's desire by setting a goals programme.*

## Ethics

What if you could fulfil your highest ideals?

Many times in my childhood, and later in my youth, I would hear my friends drift into discussion about their ideals and principles in relation to the adult world and what they would do about achieving these ideals if they were adults. Youth is a wonderful time of hope. But it is unfortunate most of us leave our childhood ideals of fairness, hope and justice back in those years of big dreams when all problems — if you were an adult — were solvable.

The fact is, many of them are still solvable, with the application of high ideals and simple logic. But failure, reinforced very often by adults, wore us down and squashed our potential. From my childhood and throughout my youth I listened to the dreams of my peers. But, alas, I never saw evidence of achievement. Why not disturb the slumber of those youthful ideas and weld them with the knowledge you have gained since? Take them a few pegs higher and consider their attainment today in the world of business, education and politics. You will find in reawakening your highest ideals you are going to open up other areas of thought long since forgotten and they will become commitments; a new you will begin to emerge forged from childhood dreams.

### Pointers
→ 1. *Your highest ideal is your best you.*
→ 2. *Take past youthful ideals and weld them to current knowledge.*
→ 3. *Open up new thoughts and ideas and peg them higher.*

## Personality

What if you could choose your own style?

I have described style in a previous chapter in this book. Style is really just a matter of choice. Who among us would not want to choose the style in part or in whole of someone we admire? Oh, to have the dignity and style exhibited by royalty, the confidence and posture of a great statesman, or the grace of a dancer or presence of a dramatic actor! Why not describe your own style in posture, voice and appearance? What would be the highest and best form you could ever devise? Would you like to be able to comfort the distressed like a wise, compassionate pastor or put across your ideas like a highly-skilled salesman or an entrepreneur? If you knew you could not fail, how far would you go in your requirements and what would you leave out? Why don't you list the attributes you see as your choice in style, even as far as detailing the kind of deliberate walk you want and the distinctive voice you require? My friends say they can always tell when I am on television (even when they are not looking), because my voice is distinctive and clear. It did not happen by accident. I was not born with a cultured voice. It was produced by deliberate design and by continual practice every morning for five years with a style in mind, a time frame set for its acquisition, and the demands of pitch, pause and projection as my constant companions until it became part of me.

We are really talking about personality because how you project yourself is how others see and respond to you. Again, in this area of life you have the absolute power of choice. In fact, you can have whatever style you want because it is guaranteed by your choice. Why not consider this aspect of style or personality — visual and audible —as part of your life goal and give it priority relative to your other goals for life?

We are really setting a pattern of personal clarification that will become our goals. You already have your own individual style, formed partly by your own personality and partly by picking up habits and postures from others. So why not *choose* your style to complement your other goals and be the best that you can?

**Pointers**
→ 1. *Your style is your choice.*
→ 2. *Your style can be programmed.*
→ 3. *Your style is the you that you want to be.*

**Guaranteed success**
What would you do if you could guarantee success? The answer to this question will almost explode your mind when you consider its possibilities. To swim the biggest river, to climb the tallest mountain, to be a billionaire or to achieve fame, recognition or even immortality flood into the mind. In the last few pages, we have asked three questions: "What if you could achieve your heart's desire?" — which refers to emotion. "What if you could fulfil your highest ideals?" — which refers to ethics. "What if you could choose your own style?" — which refers to your personality. All of these were used to stimulate and provoke attainable goals. But this question of guaranteeing success may seem, at the very least, a little far-fetched. Please stay with me on this track and let's examine the claim and bring it to reality.

Goals can be generally reached by (1) the time factor, (2) the ability required, (3) the drive by the participant, (4) the opportunity or opposition presented. *The time factor* must have first preference. It is no good setting a goal to shift a mountain by a certain date, knowing that with all the equipment and manpower available, only a small amount of dirt can be moved in an hour. The time factor must be of paramount importance and everything must work within its tightly held, unforgiving frame. So your goal, anyone's goal, must respect the confines of time. On that basis we all compete evenly.

*The second factor* is somewhat different because your ability depends very often on the amount that has to be learned and your commitment to it. But again we all have to reach our goals on this basis and all of us can do it if we want to.

*The third factor* deals with the intangible item called drive, and can only be measured by demonstration. Given that we have normal physical and mental abilities, the task ahead is our personal responsibility. Again, we are all in the same boat.

*The fourth requirement* again depends on personal choice. Some will take opportunities that others will not. Likewise, opposition will be avoided by some and induced by others. What I am really saying here is we are all given a fair share. It is like a democracy, where the free enterprise system is encouraged. It is here that you can choose your own goal and plan to reach it with some definite degree of certainty. So, bearing in mind the four laws of goal setting suggested for you, if you could guarantee success, what would you choose?

Remember the earlier advice. Think big and break out of the dream cocoon, then document the goal to give it permanence. Selection of your goals can only be made by you for your own life to give you the power and drive to achieve them.

## Pointers
→ 1. *All goals have a time factor restriction.*
→ 2. *All goals require identifiable ability.*
→ 3. *All goals require the participant's drive.*
→ 4. *All goals face both opportunity and opposition.*

CHAPTER NINE

# Some Fallacies About Goal Orientation

# CHAPTER NINE

# Some Fallacies About Goal Orientation

**Your family**

I suppose the most persistent question I am asked about my life is, "How much time do you spend with your family?" I usually respond with the answer, "More than you do!" A common fallacy is that a highly, goal-orientated person is hard on his family. Yet the opposite generally applies. When you set goals for life, you include things you want to do as well as things you do not want to do. One of my objectives has always been that I will maintain a strong, close family life, even after the children are married. It is interesting, now that they are all married, that the goal has been maintained and the rewards are indescribable.

Some people find it hard to believe, but I almost never take any work home or discuss my work at home, because that's how I arranged my goals programme. It allows for a close family life. Even in travel I endeavour to keep my time away short and to keep in phone contact regularly. Wherever possible, my wife and I travel together.

To suggest that you may disadvantage your family by a goals programme is displaying an active ignorance as to what a goals programme can do for them. If there is one thing that keeps a marriage harmonious, it is security. And security comes more from planning than by accident. A life goal that includes the responsibilities of family life — for life — is another example of parental and matrimonial love that says in a very meaningful way, "I love you and care for you." When the honeymoon is over, and tensions and disagreements occur, there is nothing more assuring to know than that a plan has been formulated that includes the whole family for mutual support and benefit.

The interesting thing I have found is that even when your children grow up and get married and you have grandchildren, the process continues because the family has accepted and appreciated the benefits of life goals. A particular goal in family life can be the arranging of picnics, or barbeques, or other occasions that provide opportunities to get together and keep lines of communication open. We purchased a small farm with a cottage and sheep, cattle and horses, so for a number of years, while the children were going through their adolescence, they could use their new-found energies and frustrations in a positive way by riding horses, repairing fences and driving tractors. The farm also allowed us to live — on weekends — apart from the world, and enjoy our evenings together around a big log fire, talking and laughing together. So that I could sleep in a little late on the first morning of a weekend at the farm, we had a simple rule: nobody made any noise or got up before me, to allow me to replenish my energy. Then I would give everybody toast and coffee in bed!

A life goal, dare I say, would be of less value without a family goal because of the great gift of family life and the strength attained from it.

**Pointers**
→ 1. *Family goals express love.*

→ 2. *Family goals give security.*
→ 3. *Family goals keep you together.*

## Compassion

To have a life-long goal-setting programme necessarily excludes some things and some people. Because you set goals which are specific and in time frames, it is impossible to work in other areas. As you set your goals in one direction, you will inevitably bypass other things that could be done and find yourself rejecting and refusing proposals and requests. As a result, you may be accused of lacking in compassion or being uncaring. You are not. The simple fact is that *to fit in to someone else's project will violate your own commitment.* This is a tough nut to crack and at times a real problem with which to come to grips. You will find you cannot make others see your point of view while they are trying to make you see theirs! But do not think that I am suggesting that your life goals programme should be so tight and inflexible that it is impossible to fit anything additional in that is worthwhile. *The key to a successful life goal is to allow time to support others.*

And at times, of course, there is the acute emergency requiring immediate attention. You must exercise your own conscience before God on these issues. Remember, sometimes we only get one chance during a lifetime to help someone in extreme need. To neglect such an opportunity may unsettle us for the rest of our lives. But once the crisis is past, back to the goals programme. As I have mentioned before, there are some things you should be prepared to lose your life's goal over. But that is rare. In most cases it may just be a big hiccup, a postponement. (And at times such major events and additional pressure can do wonders for reassessment). Life goals must have within their boundaries compassionate causes that make you think and feel beyond yourself. Select compassionate causes carefully and allow for additional time and expertise to be made available.

### Pointers
→ 1. *Life goals must have openings for unexpected compassionate calls.*
→ 2. *Life goals can programme compassionate involvement.*
→ 3. *Life goals prepare you to do good for others.*

## Selfishness

It is very easy to focus on your life goals with daily affirmations and still be quite selfish. Someone once said, a man can be so busy making a living that he fails to make a life. But you don't have to be selfish. I average about one speaking appointment each week and I deal with a considerable amount of mail answering people's problems. I also generally have appointments with individuals each week who are seeking help. At these times I make sure I give as much of myself as possible. *There is no substitute for sharing yourself with others.* In person, you open the door of your heart, which helps you feel as others feel. Financially, of course, we really ought to give and give generously. Do not wait to hit the pay dirt before giving, but make it part of your daily existence to be generous.

Many people talk about giving their time, or their expertise as a proxy for giving money. But there is something quite magical that happens to a person's spirit when they can give hard cash continually and consistently throughout their life — in good times and in bad.

The giving of cash, expertise, information and, above all, ourselves is probably the hardest thing to do, and the way in which we rationalise the amount and its frequency is a dynamic illustration of that fact. (If you want to undertake a serious study of that area, read *How to be Happy Though Rich*).

Goals for life that include giving provide the joy that

keeps us going.

**Pointers**
→ 1. *Programme selfless acts which involve you personally.*
→ 2. *Give without trading.*
→ 3. *Give consistently.*

## Criticism

All of us have at one time or another felt the sting of criticism — the injustice of it and the uncertainty of it. Criticism is as sure as death and taxes. While it will be impossible to avoid criticism, I warn you here and now to expect more of it as you consider goals for life. There are four basic reasons why you can expect to be criticised more in the future. I will list them so that you can be prepared.

1. *You will be criticised because you are not conforming to normal behaviour.* Once you set goals for life, with the inherent objectives and obligations, you step away from the crowd; you have broken with conformity.

2. *Criticism comes from possessing dreams and purpose which guide and direct your life.* Here you will encounter envy because your life goals are obviously having an effect on you. Your motivation will often be described as arrogance, pride and even ruthlessness. And to know where you are going, and how you are going to get there, poses a threat to those who get along by going along.

3. *Your objective planning and motivation mirrors the inadequacy of the critic.* Most people know they can do better and when you confront them with a life which is growing and expanding it will not go unnoticed and you will be pulled down.

4. *You will attract criticism because you have taken control of your own life and accepted personal account-*

*ability*. In taking this course of action you are suggesting others do the same. You are challenging and provoking them. You will attract criticism.

**Pointers**
→ 1. *Remember the biggest critic generally does the least work.*
→ 2. *Paying attention to your critics validates their claim and elevates them.*
→ 3. *Ignoring your critics saves time and energy.*
→ 4. *Never criticise a critic.*

## Don't be side-tracked

Suddenly your circumstances change, by a recession, bereavement, a crisis or what looks like a great opportunity. The circumstances, if they get your attention, are generally unusual in content and timing, so be careful about getting side-tracked. Circumstances that side-track us from the main course usually do so in a minor way at first, then, by pseudo-rationalisation, we pursue that path only to find we are far from our original objective and have wasted time, energy and money.

There will always crop up special circumstances that seek our attention and if pursued, will absorb our energy and thwart our progress. The way to avoid this is to have a list of qualifications before you allow circumstances to invade your goals programme. There are occasions when new circumstances actually provide an entrance into a goals programme because of their proximity to your aims. But be careful and examine anything that comes by unplanned circumstance. Make sure it provides an alternative route to the path you have already prepared.

*Enforced goals.* While you are scrambling for a foothold to continue with your goals programme, you may have goals actually forced on you. An example could be an increase in interest rates which is far above your budget. Suddenly your cash flow is upset. So you now have an additional goal you cannot avoid. How do you handle that kind of situation?

The answer is with careful thought and positive action. The evaluation must take into consideration the deadlines that must be met. If it is long-term or urgent-term, then a revised goal must be immediately created by formulating a plan, with all the required checkpoints, increasing the size of the goal to meet the demand. Be careful that enforced goals don't take you off the track — keep them in perspective.

*Subconscious goals.* The subconscious can play tricks with us. When we have set a deliberate course of action with all of the qualifications and time frames, every now and then we sabotage ourselves with bad behaviour or bad decisions. Sometimes we have guilty feelings or attitudes because of something we did or didn't do some time earlier. We overlooked it or did not clear it up earlier. At such a time, you need to go back to the first chapter and re-check and re-affirm your value system. Re-read chapter one with complete honesty and clarity. This is because your subsconscious may not be in tune with your conscious thinking. So conflict occurs.

What is happening is the subsconscious mind is trying to pursue entirely different goals to what you have formulated for your life and these must be corrected. Likewise, examine your subsconscious for signals in case you're on the wrong track. The subsconscious mind has the facilities of a miraculous filing cabinet and can, in a flash, go over years of experience, picking up thoughts here and there to form an answer or opinion on any subject. So treat it with respect.

*Tentative goals.* Sometimes we set goals tentatively as a means of testing the waters before the big plunge. We should do this infrequently because it can become habit forming and prevent us from using our dream machine for role playing as well as make us lazy in seeking full and helpful information. To use a tentative goal indicates uncertainty and when we are unsure, we tend to hold back some of our energies and commitment levels. After a while, tentative goals may become a way of life which restricts us and holds us back for greater things. Life goals cannot be tentative, they must have the sure, firm seal of commitment. Tentative goals are for tentative people and tentative situations. Make sure that they are used in proper context for rare situations.

*Ego goals.* As I watched a television interview with an executive from a giant corporation which had just crashed, I heard the interviewer ask why a particular incident caused the collapse of this great industrial empire. The Chief Executive responded, rather bravely I thought, "My ego got in the way!"

To promote ego goals is probably the most dangerous of the side-track goals because, as with King Midas, the craving for more and more does nothing to satisfy the appetite. I have been in the presence of many leaders and listened to their entourage tell them only that which they wanted to hear. This distances a leader from the position of leadership to driftsmanship.

Many have fallen or failed to reach their life goals because their ego got in the way and demanded more space until the life goal collapsed for want of attention. I am not suggesting that a big ego is wrong, but I am suggesting that an ego out of control is wrong. By out of control I mean becoming the object of the life goal or pulling down the life goal to gain prominence.

Our total life must be under control and that is why, earlier in this book, I expressed my commitment to the Christian gospel which elevates Jesus Christ and His principles. In following Him, I also will be elevated to my highest potential.

**Pointers**
→ 1. *Don't be side-tracked by sabotaging goals.*
→ 2. *Don't be side-tracked by pseudo-rationalisation*

*of new circumstances.*

→ 3. *Don't let your lust for recognition side-track you.*

# The Goals Formula

# CHAPTER TEN

# The Goals Formula

**Clear definition**

Just as there are laws relating to physics, there are ground rules for goal-setters. You break those rules at your peril. Keep those laws and you will succeed. In this chapter, I will outline seven major guidelines.

Most of the groundwork towards establishing life goals has been covered in previous chapters. It is time now to develop detailed information on your life goals and definitions. Definitions must include all categories of importance: family life, finance, social life, religion, giving and the support of your country. The world will keep on going without you, but you cannot keep going without involvement in the world. Quite simply, if you become a cold, calculating, single-minded, objective-oriented person without relating to circumstances around you, in the process of reaching your goals, you will isolate yourself from humanity itself.

So rule one is: *clearly define your life goals in terms of ultimate achievement*. It may well be that you have cleared away all the superfluous padding already and got down to a concise description of what you are really

aiming for. In the previous chapters I have suggested that
free flow of thought and the continuance of words with
embellishments will help you to stretch your mind and
activate your imagination. At this point we must remove
the embellishments and tighten our description in an
effort to get closer to our life goals, both in definition and
priority.

Remember the clearer and more complete your
definition, the easier it is for you to relate to goals at any
moment and the easier it is to measure any new
opportunity. To write out your life goal will be difficult
because of the enormous commitment level embodied in
the overall plan. You are, in fact, trading your unknown
future for a confirmed future. While on the surface it
appears to be a simple and logical trade, you may find
deep down you would still like the chance to let go and
leave it all to circumstance. Your strong resolve at this
point must be committed to paper and your life goal will
only become reality as you write it down as a simple,
logical statement of faith.

I carry my life goal with me always so I can affirm its
charter against anything I do, and because it is enhanced
by written clarity, I can, within a moment, evaluate
almost any decision against it. *Your life goal should
consist of one thing*, and being one item, it will provide a
clear description for all else to conform to it. My own life
goal is confined to just a few lines of writing and, although
I have memorised it, I still read it daily for affirmation and
motivation.

The next step is to define the major supportive goals
which thrust a life goal onward to the summit. Those
goals may be numerous, but each will play a major role in
the overall plan. Let me illustrate. I have one life goal but I
have twenty-nine major secondary goals that support it
either directly or indirectly. My goals relating to my
family may not directly relate to the total attainment of
my life goal, but what a sad day it would be if I reached the

summit and lost my greatest asset, which is my family.

There are some major goals relating to books which I want to write, and groups I want to help, which, if not achieved, could be compensated for by large results in other areas. But, I would still reach my life goal. Other goals are so inter-locked with my ultimate life goal that I must achieve each one in sequence. The key is the stability of your life goal, in tangible form. Your supportive goals also need clarity and documentation to complete the picture.

The final step to achieving your life goal is to define your minor goals. These are areas of your life that can be dealt with with a minimum of fuss. Rarely would a minor goal extend past two years, and if it did, it would be a routine item requiring the input of time rather than heavy or consistent effort.

Your definition of your life goals must now be in the form of a simple written document, expressing in clear terms your life goal, your major supportive goals — with a clear description of each one — and your minor goals, which support your major goals.

*Be prepared to spend prime time completing this task, because you are going to trade your life for it* in one form or another. Go backwards and forwards over your written description, polishing and pruning where necessary so that the final document paints word pictures of such clarity and purpose you feel any change at all would mar the masterpiece.

### Pointers
→ 1. *Describe in clear terms your life goal.*
→ 2. *Describe your subordinate major goals.*
→ 3. *Describe subordinate minor goals.*

## Goal strategy
It is one thing to set out your life goals in descriptive terms and look at them with satisfaction, but it is

something else to say in clear detailed terms how you are going to do it. Obviously the life goal must come first, as it is the overwhelming purpose of your life. The second rule is, *set out your strategy*. The strategy here is both simple and involved. It is simple because of its definition and its time frame, but involved in its ultimate attainment. I have set my life goals' attainment at 85 years of age because I believe this is a reasonable time frame for its realisation. This does not limit my life or goal — both can be expanded — but for the sake of having something to aim at, I set the goal and its supportive goals to fit into this particular time bracket. I have made allowances in my life goal for expansion should I be blessed with more years than I expect. My life goal is predicated on a measurement of attainment in a specific area of life directly controlled and influenced by my Christian commitment.

My life goal is too personal to declare to others in its entirety, but I share with some selected people its general destiny and course. For my own purpose, I have reduced my life goal into units so that I can measure progress. This means I can strategise because I can regulate with realistic and uniform measurement. If you cannot find a measurement to guide your strategy, then you will not know how far you have travelled, and if you don't know how far you have travelled then you do not know how far you have to go. Confusion begins and goals lose their sharpness.

With my life goals, I strategise with respect to the educational tools and physical requirements that I need to develop to give me the endurance to complete the task. The other requirement is style, which I covered in the earlier chapters. This really gives an emphasis on quality in the years of attainment. Having defined your life goal strategy in a general way, it is time to go straight to the bottom of the pile and look at your foundation goals that provide a solid base to build on. Remember to allocate the most effort to the early years and to foundation building, to prevent an unexpected collapse later, because here you are sharpening your skills.

Whatever happens, do not get impatient or despondent because you see little change or response to the outlay of thought and energy. In later years you are going to be just as amazed at the quantum leaps you make with seemingly little or no effort. Plan every detail of what you need. Determine its purpose and how it fits into your overall plan. The major goals must, of course, fit into the life goal and yet the substance of the life goal — if it is going to be effective in motivation — must be seen in form and function as you go along. As you work and plan in these areas you will see a pattern form, and each part of the jigsaw enhances the picture.

Your minor goals also must be attended to, fitting into the major goals to create the total picture of a life plan. The exercises in the previous chapters have prepared your mind for the planning of your goals. Make sure you have special milestones or events that emphasise your arrival at particular destinations in your life. If that is impractical, remember the measurement of units and use that to recognise a level of achievement.

### Pointers
→ 1. *Strategy creates energy.*
→ 2. *Strategy saves energy.*
→ 3. *Strategy gives direction.*

## Planning out the problems
Every long-term plan and every life goal has problem areas which need to be dealt with. How you react to these problems is going to either increase or decrease the way in which they will be solved. To expect the problems to be solved as you go along is unrealistic. Why not *plan out the problem areas* before you commence your life goal's programme?

The first problem is always personal and usually has to do with attitudes of belief and commitment. It is at the personal problem level of attitude that the task can become easier if a few simple rules are observed. Problems are always a growth experience: as we tackle the problem areas of our own attitude, and succeed, the biggest and most worthwhile victories are won. Take another look at yourself and identify the personal areas of dissatisfaction. Place into your goals' programme, at whatever level you can accept as being correct, a method to root out the problem areas with the personal equipment available. Most people start out in business or on a goals' programme under-capitalised, and generally think this is the greatest limiting factor they could possibly have. Yet the business experience has shown that those who start out with huge amounts of capital generally lose it, and in a very short time.

Large capital amounts are not necessary, but large capital plans are. The financial areas of your total life plans need to be attended to probably more than anything else. If you search out the financial problem areas you will save enormous amounts of time and anguish with respect to your long and short term performance. Examine the obstacles that stand in the way of you reaching your life goal and they will probably fall into one of three areas.

Number one is personal, these are problems in relation to belief, attitude and discipline and usually are the most difficult to plan out because of the deep thought and harsh investigation required. The earlier chapters regarding a value system should have dealt with that area.

Number two is financial. Everybody thinks their financial problems are in the realm of the "too little" rather than the "too much." Yet a tight budget always teaches resourcefulness and ideas, while a more comfortable budget can encourage slothfulness and keep us in a comfort zone. Plan your finances carefully and calculate your needs to prevent cash blow-outs, which could collapse your goals structure and bring you back to the starting line with a thud. Do not underestimate the care needed on financial matters and document your income and your expenditure as a matter of fact, rather than fiction.

Number three is logistical. It may well be that you have decided you are not in the right place at the right time or that you need to get closer to the action if you are going to reach the apex of your life goal. I deliberately moved home from the suburbs to a park setting in the centre of the city to save time and body stress. I estimated I averaged up to eight hours a week travelling to my office, which accounts for seven-and-a-half weeks a year sitting behind the wheel of a car! This did not equate with my life goals' programme of achievement and growth. Plan your location and movements with respect to your home, place of business, access to national and international flights or whatever your logistical requirements are. Plan out the obstacles that stand in your way.

### Pointers
→ 1. *Problems can be planned out.*
→ 2. *The biggest problem is your attitude.*
→ 3. *Failure to plan is failure to man.*

## Building in reserves
The fourth rule is, *build in reserves*. There is a great deal of talk today about "burn-out" and many people are forced to rest — even to the point of hospitalisation. What makes an intelligent human being continue to work regardless of the consequences, ignoring mental and body signals with respect to his or her health?

No army general will continue to drive his men without due regard for their well-being, because the consequence of such an action could very easily give the enemy the edge. I am not suggesting a coasting along or a six-month-holiday-twice-a-year. I am suggesting intelligent reserves for your body, mind and spirit. I rarely take any work home because that is my haven from the world and that is where I read, reflect and fortify. How else could I go year after year without holidays or rest periods? My method is to get to bed as early as I can, as often as I can, and to obtain stress relief by riding horses or having a massage or a sauna. I try to do those things on a regular basis, so even though I work hard and continuously, I always have reserves.

If you're going to make a mark in life it is going to be a long haul and you are going to have to build in powerful reserves to hedge you against unexpected opportunities and reversals. The most important reserves are mental, particularly in the area of self confidence, and affirmations that you are on the right track, and totally committed to a life goal's programme. I continually read biographies and autobiographies as encouragement to my own spirit. By reading of the experiences of others, with their victories and their misadventures, I can build my confidence reserves, ever ready in case of a calamity or an unusual opportunity.

The other area where reserves are required is with people, and those reserves must be planned. During difficult periods in your life, when you have your back to the wall, and information or help is required, very often it is not what you know but who you know.

Build into your life goals *people reserves* in different areas of concern and need. Obviously, this means planning and selectivity with mutual respect. In so doing your own life is protected and your life goals protected by a kind of insurance policy of people in case of trouble. It is amazing to me the number of people that call me only when they need help and usually at the most inappropriate times. They know in some way that because of my Christian call I must respond. Yet I would have to be less than honest if I did not say that I wish they would call me occasionally just as a greeting to balance the budget!

Build in people reserves as your greatest barrier against difficult situations and always try to be in the front line offering others help. It is truly more blessed to give than to receive.

I have a few words in my goals' programme that read: "I will always keep sensible cash reserves." I strive to have a benchmark of fluid financial reserves to protect my family and my life goals' programme against the unexpected events of this world. Just imagine, if you will, that you are ten years down the track towards your life goal and a recession hits upon your business or even your country. How then will a life goals' programme be continued without some financial reserves? I have noticed with unhappy regularity the number of organisations that collapse because they lack strong financial reserves. Yet it seems inevitable from time to time that businesses, industry and government have recessions. Those who survive it are usually bigger, better and stronger, while those who are not prepared for it either close or reduce in size and lose their effectiveness. Take care to ensure your financial assets are solid and not the type that can be worth a fortune one day and worthless the next. Also make sure that your assets are inflation-proof and will minimise taxation requirements; otherwise at your hour of need your resources may be restricted.

In preparing your simple life goals' formula, build in reserves, not to provide a comfort zone of complacency, but rather a battle zone for survival enabling you to continue and stretch your real life goal.

## Pointers
→ 1. *Mental, physical and spiritual reserves are good sense.*
→ 2. *People in key positions are strong reserves.*
→ 3. *Financially fluid assets are necessary protective reserves.*

## Relating to time frames

I am often amused by people who say they are determined to do something and then fail to put the target of their determination into a time frame. The very word "determination" embodies the word terminate, which expresses the full meaning of the word. All your dreams, desires, ideals and goals are but a vapour without the strong, firm, searching eyes of finalisation. So rule five is, *everything that you have stressed inwardly or on paper during your progress through this book needs to be examined against and within a limited time frame.*

If you are contemplating some grand scheme for your life, (and I hope you are), then such a plan must focus itself upon your life goal within a reasonable life span. Should your plan not reasonably fit into the balance of your life, then it must be altered to conform. I am not for one moment suggesting a reduction of your life plan, but rather a revision and examination to allow for more to be done in less time. Now is the time to examine in detail, and within practical terms, your additional educational requirements, to allow if need be, a time frame for study and examination. It may pay to do several things at once if you are faced with institutionalised time frames, otherwise the progress in that area could drag behind the progress in other areas which will unnecessarily limit you.

Evaluate time frames and allow for planning because new information, and changes in world and local events, may add different measurements of pressure in different directions. The life goal programme must be laid out carefully against your major and minor goals, individually assessed with careful, informative feedback for completion and then programmed into the over-all plan. The programming must allow for delays or early achievement, with alternatives, so no time will be wasted by delays or early arrivals. Some of your goals may only commence when others are finished. Then other requirements may have to be slotted in while others may have to be planned out. The life goal is immovable. The other goals are the tools to support the attainment of the ultimate objective. Relate to time frames so that both pressured and less pressured goals are patterned. This enables an allocation of energy. Remember, we are talking of a long haul and, while it is important to expend much effort launching the programme, a continuity of pressure will result in fuzzy thinking and treadmill activity. Consider also the completion of a part of your total programme and document its occurrence along with what your thoughts and responses are. This will give you encouragement to press on. Remember that the end of each goal becomes the beginning of another. After a while each new beginning will seem to require less energy because your success ratio will improve and you will better understand the process.

Take some time to write down each goal on a piece of paper and spread each goal out on a desk over a time frame map representing your life. Then move each one around until the pattern is completed to your satisfaction. At the risk of repeating myself too much, I have to emphasise that ample time must be given to the demands of change. Be aware that a change does not represent an opportunity just to avoid pressure or commitment. I went broke three times over a five year period, stayed in sub-standard hotels and drove sometimes for days on hot, dusty, unmade roads. But rather than getting closer to my tangible goals, I was becoming further removed from them! However, during that period I was being equipped mentally and spiritually for a huge quantum jump that only became available because of my disappointments in the past. What really happened was that I became a different person during those five years, and the experiences and knowledge that I gained, prepared me well to recognise a good opportunity and gave me the ability to handle it.

**Pointers**
→ 1. *Express each goal in a time frame.*
→ 2. *Mix suitable goals in the same time frame.*
→ 3. *All goals must fit into time frames.*

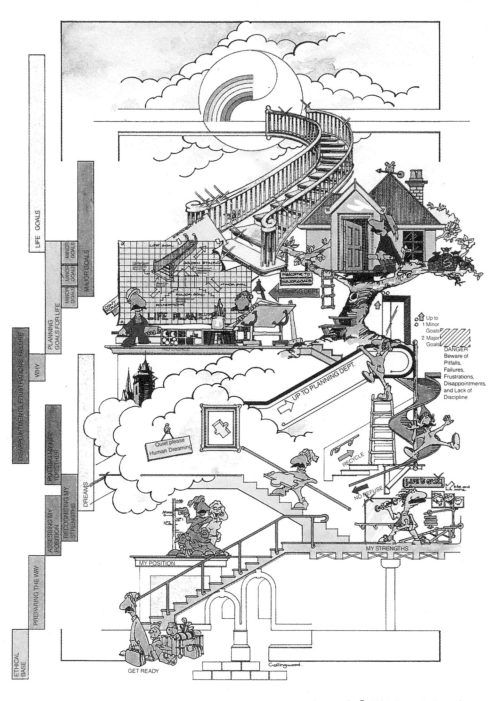

# Ground rules for goal setters — the Goal Formula

**Create a master plan**

Now is the time for the finale in respect to setting and solidifying our life goals, and their supportive structures. We have separately dealt with each area in the "Goal Formula," and all of these must now be welded into a master plan for achievement. You may have considered covering each of the areas in the goals' formula on a different coloured sheet of paper and putting them in a folder for easy access with indexed subjects. This one — number six — is the ultimate master plan and should be made distinctive by way of its layout.

There also must be space allowed to write in comments and progress with starting and completion dates included. All goals, strategy, problems, reserves and time frames must now mesh and harmonise with each other. The foundation stones which represent your commencement goals must dovetail with supportive goals and the life goal to complete the picture. The strategies must mix and match so that no goal is in conflict with another, causing a waste of energy.

Try and work out areas of common ground in your strategy which, for very little extra effort could double or triple the results simply by mixing the components.

Collectively summarise the cost of your master plan in the areas of time, money and personal freedom as well as in the less tangible areas of life, and build a word picture of such a cost. Now harmonise that cost in time frames. It will be necessary to protect your progress by including in your master plan checkpoints for attainment and what other scores need to be reached before moving on. Discipline will be necessary to prevent moving ahead on a more enjoyable part of your plan before catching up with other areas which may not be as fulfilling. Also, make sure your financial and other reserves are in place. Don't even move without that point being clear.

The longer you progress in your life goals' programme the more you have to lose, and I am amazed at the high risks some people take just to be able to say, "I got there early." Keep your reserves for setbacks; do not use them for a leap forward in case of emergency problems. This part of your life goals' planning is probably the hardest because it requires you to think again through every area of your plans and re-dream your dreams enabling them to be put into workable plans related to hard facts, time frames, finance and normal human restraints.

Do not forget the lessons of the earlier chapters on "Achievement," and particularly the Biblical charge, "as a man thinketh in his heart, so is he!" From this we begin to get the picture, from God's point of view, that we literally become what we think about. Psychological and behavioural science also confirms that fact. Whatever you do, don't flush out with facts the dream areas of your life goals, or limit in any way your ability to grow and to do. Rather, put them in harmony with the five main areas of the Goal Formula. Do not limit their impact or scope, but place them in a framework that will give opportunity for the unexpected break-through, and, at the same time, protect you against the harshness and destruction of an unexpected difficulty or catastrophe. What you are doing is summarising all the loose ends and blending them together to form a predictable plan for your life. *Days, weeks and even months spent on clarification of this plan will not only save you years of work but much pain. Remember, the plan does not do the work for you!* You do that yourself! What the plan does is point the way and identify the tools. It is up to you to provide the motivation, wisdom and stickability in getting there.

**Pointers**
→ 1. *Summarise the formula.*
→ 2. *Harmonise all plans.*
→ 3. *Protect your progress with checkpoints.*

---

**RULE 1:** Clearly define your goals

**RULE 2:** Set out your strategy

**RULE 3:** Plan out the problems

**RULE 4:** Build in reserves

**RULE 5:** Relate everything to a time frame

**RULE 6:** Create a master plan

**RULE 7:** Actionize it now

---

**Actionize it now**

No great achievement can be realised without action and so it is with goal setting.

Theories are great — knowledge can be power — good intentions are only weak promises. But decisive action can turn the smallest dream into a magnificent reality.

So actionize your goal promptly and provoke it by action continually and in doing so you will fulfill your life's goal.

# CHAPTER ELEVEN

# How To Maintain Your Goals

# How To Maintain
# Your Goals

## Attention to detail

As I move from city to city and country to country I am forever looking out for ideas and differences. In particular I notice the areas in which men and women excel as separate groups — which, in my opinion, proves again that the differences between the sexes are more than biological. I was making enquiries in a travel organisation when I noticed that all the staff in the office were women. I said to the senior female executive, "I know why there are no men in this office." She asked me why. I replied, "You have women here because they can handle repetitious work and pay attention to detail." She agreed.

The hardest job I have found in all business life is to get men to pay attention to detail. On the other hand, one of my other difficulties is getting women to stop majoring on minor issues. It seems to me that to get a combination of the best of both sexes — that is, to get a woman to see the big picture and to get men to handle detail — is very difficult, although not impossible. When you get a combination of both, you have a powerful, persuasive and capable person. I believe that the skill of seeing the full picture can be acquired just as attention to detail can be acquired.

I remember well the frustration my son, Peter, caused in our office because he would not complete the details, and follow up documentation of sales, during the early years. It was so bad that I very nearly lost my best female senior executive over it. Today Peter is a complete professional and I doubt whether it would be possible for any one to handle detail any better than he. What caused the change was a simple law: *If you don't inspect you cannot expect.* Peter found himself forever chasing up old sales and patching up what he thought was completed work. In other words, he found it more profitable, financially and for peace of mind, to finish the job to the last detail. He learned to ask questions and seek out information before, during and after the sale to ensure that it all proceeded with a minimum of fuss. The results were remarkable. His new habits have expressed themselves in returns in many different ways.

At times we must ask the seemingly silly question and sometimes seek out more information than we need so we are not caught on the hop. I am not suggesting we become paranoid, but we do need to check, double-check and sometimes check again. Also we need to get people to repeat instructions to make sure they understand. Some years ago I was faced with a situation in business where I could not get clients to respond to our correspondence. As is the custom in my organisation, from time to time I read out-going correspondence. Suddenly I saw the problem. I met with our office staff and I asked one employee if she could give me a time frame for the phrase "as soon as possible." She said, "Well it really depends on the person's circumstances and the urgency factor that they see in the request." I then asked another staff member to respond to the question, "Could you contact this office at your earliest convenience." Again I received a response that was quite ambiguous. I then asked another staff member to respond to the request, "Could you contact our office urgently?" He said he would expect a response within a week or so. I'm sure you can see what I'm getting at. I changed all that by getting all staff to send out correspondence with a date for expected reply and a diary entry for immediate follow up if no reply was forthcoming. The result was startling because people respond to clear instruction and advice. *The amount of work created by a mistake usually requires four times the amount of time required to do it right.* I saw an unforgettable cartoon on the wall of an executive suite. The caption said it all: "Measure twice and saw it once." Good advice! Attention to detail will put you light-years ahead of others, and if you make the same mistake twice, remember it so it will never happen again.

### Pointers
→ 1. *Attention to detail can be learned.*
→ 2. *Inspect what you expect.*
→ 3. *When you make the same mistake twice, remember it.*

## Daily affirmation
Keeping track of life goals requires diligence and perseverance. Concentration can easily be fragmented and the problems of life that beset us all from time to time can seem overwhelming. Before we know where we are, our goals are forgotten and our dreams smashed. I have found that daily, weekly and monthly affirmations keep me on the track and provide, in a very real way, motivation and growth. I have, in written form, my life goals in detail with my 29 major goals in chronological order with supportive helps and minor goals up until my 85th birthday. To have that in written form is in itself something of a success in planning. But what if I put it under lock and key and only return to it on my 85th birthday for evaluation? Do you think I would be able to

arrive on time and keep that which I have committed?

I read my life goals every morning and confirm my major goals every week. I write a letter to myself every month explaining where I am in relation to my goals. The interesting thing here is that I then have a look at the letter I wrote to myself twelve or fifteen months ago and compare it with what has happened since. I then find out where I have lied! My experience is that unless we keep short accounts with ourselves in respect to affirmation and progress, we falter and start to make excuses. Then our self esteem suffers because we lose our integrity. I measure every single day, giving 25 points for simplicity; 25 points for desperation; 25 points for planning and 25 points for daily achievements. This way I can keep close watch on my standard of performance. (For more detailed information on daily assessment, read my book *How To Be Happy Though Rich*.)

Keep loose leaves or extra pages in your goals book to allow for the addition of quick ideas you can enter from time to time which will enhance your programme. I believe this technique of writing in a book everything I have done well in life gives me the added boost I need when faced with a large challenge or a difficult situation. The Bible does say in Philippians, "Whatever things are true, noble, right, pure, lovely and admirable, think of these things.' (Philippians 4:8). I am very conscious of the negativity surrounding us all, and the desperate need to repel that influence with positive affirmation. So I am suggesting that you write down all the things you do well and read them on occasions when you feel negativity is creeping in. The other simple thing I have is a small card with a reduced photograph on it of everything which must be done for the next ten years. I keep this in my pocket for easy reference to check progress and evaluate anything suggested to me. In this way I ensure that it fits in with my life goal plans.

Affirmation also means mixing with people who are

achievers and always looking for the individual who can do something better than you, so that you can learn from them. Good books are on the market continually with new techniques and interesting stories of how other people either did great things or developed theories of suggested ways things can be done. Avoid those who are forever complaining and pouring out negative thoughts. I have found it takes a great deal more positive input to overcome negative input. It is almost as if you have to stand sentinel at the gate of your mind and challenge thoughts as they come to you for negative or positive charge!

Try and spend one hour a week going over your goals programme, measuring performance and planning the next move. The more time you spend affirming your goals, the more a part of you they become. But do not substitute paper action for proper action or activity for objectivity.

### Pointers
→ 1. *Affirm your goal daily.*
→ 2. *Have a ten-year goal card in your wallet.*
→ 3. *Create a book on things you have done well.*

### Expand as you go
As the clouds of limitation lift and new horizons of growth present a wider picture, then is the time to expand your goals. All of us, however much we dream or project, cannot accurately predict our final growth rate. The bondage of past and present restraints crowd our thoughts, and our thoughts in turn provide our goals. So we must have goals that are expandable in kind and in direction. For instance, it may be your ultimate life goal is to develop the biggest and most successful business of its kind in your city. As your knowledge and experience grow and the years unfold, you may find that the earlier life goal has expanded. It now becomes the largest

business of its kind in the state or the nation. The focus must be on the direction you are going. The moment you lose sight of that direction, problems arise. A business in our city expanded and grew, manufacturing and distributing electrical hardware items for other manufacturing companies and retail outlets. Over the years this particular company concentrated more in a particular direction until it reached the stage of limited specialisation. The end of that company came when it tried to keep the organisation going when its specialised goods were no longer required. What had happened was it had worked itself into a limited market with limited items, so that its whole business stood or fell on one product. *So do not limit your goals in a direction that has an abrupt end.* Rather choose a direction that can include, absorb and benefit by change. Never let your life goals be changed or dictated by the major or minor goals — they are there to serve the life goal, not to set or change direction. It could be that the major or minor goals have expanded or taken a different direction over a period of time. You may even create new ones and drop some, but it is all in the purpose of serving the ultimate life goal to give it the nurture and support it needs.

### Pointers
→ 1. *As your limitations lift, so lift your goals.*
→ 2. *Be direction-orientated.*
→ 3. *Don't let major or minor goals reset direction.*

## Changing life style
As you grow and expand towards your life goal your personality will change. It is not that you have become a different person, but rather a better person because you are becoming more fulfilled. Sometimes it is hard to imagine that the change will take place, but the inevitable will occur and you will go where once you did not want to go. So you will become involved in different social and

political areas. The motor car you drive may be upgraded and the home in which you live may change or expand because your standard of living is upgraded. Because you have increased your earnings, so you are able to enjoy some material benefits. A changed life style definitely changes you, even if only in what you say and where you say it. Now you will have influence, and what you say can influence other people. So you become news, and it well may be you are even sought out for public comment. Even your vacations may take on a new and exciting meaning. No-one can take away the wonderful times we had many years ago with our children camping on the beach and the fun that we had will never be forgotten. But today, with the family grown up, our holiday could be anywhere in the world. Our lifestyle has changed. Your friends will change, not I hope, because you think you are now too sophisticated and elevated to retain old friendships, but because some will leave you over a period of time. Because of your growth and gradual change in lifestyle, some friends will be unable to accept the change. But the fact is they no longer feel comfortable with you, and you will have to come to grips with that.

Do not stunt your lifestyle by putting limitations on its growth, but maintain good manners and a respect for the individuality of others. Avoid flaunting your wealth, particularly with those less fortunate. Some friends, of course, will grow with you, and others, who really love you, will stay and enjoy with you the new lifestyle and encourage you to push on. They may even be a little proud of what their dear friend has achieved!

As your lifestyle changes, be outgoing and develop poise and etiquette for every occasion. If you are not quite sure what to do, set a minor goal to study the subject by studying books and observing what others do. It takes a certain amount of skill to entertain people graciously and make everyone feel welcome, wanted and comfortable. But a few well selected comments or questions can usually make even the most reserved and timid person feel at home. Don't feel guilty or uncomfortable about your new-found lifestyle, but rather be grateful for goals accomplished and access to more opportunities. I find it disconcerting to see seemingly good, honest Christians who have attained a degree of wealth, attempt to portray a poverty-stricken life style — refusing to talk about money and, in some respects, practising deceit to prevent demands being made upon them. We should always be mindful of the fact our growth and lifestyle will act as a model for others. It also acts as a point of judgement on our character and personality.

Make an effort to be complimentary and uplifting with friends and you will be welcome wherever you go.

### Pointers
→ 1. *Expand your lifestyle graciously.*
→ 2. *Make others feel comfortable when they are around you.*
→ 3. *Do not feel guilty about change.*

### Reaffirm your charter

There will come times during your journey towards life's goals that you will put on the brakes and question the wisdom of it all. What am I doing here? Where am I going? Am I on the right track? These times of self doubt occur as you bump into life's rough edges, or have sand kicked in your face once too often. I often ask myself that question. This is the time to reflect quickly on past achievements. The victories I attained were because I accepted my life goals charter and pushed on regardless. As you complete certain milestones in your life, you will rise above your old self and expand what you thought were limiting factors. It is good to reaffirm your goals. Reaffirming your charter is necessary because you are probably now in a comfort zone and, having endured some pain to reach that zone, reaffirmation is required to endure more and complete the course. What a sad picture we would be if we reached a comfort zone somewhere on the way to a life goal and we dwelt there too long, only to find towards the end of life we had failed to complete the course. Having failed because of difficulties is one thing, but having failed because of unwillingness, is something quite different.

In reaffirming your charter, it is wise to investigate new advances in technology and new techniques which will give new life to old ideas, particularly, and more often, after you pass the halfway mark. The temptation to wander will be strong at that point. The easiest way to find out whether you are starting to slip into a rut is to observe how often you talk about what you have done in the past rather than what more you have to do in the future. In other words, you need a futuristic outlook, to stay on the track.

If you find you are losing your hunger to grow and your charter has lost its bloom, then move into younger company where people are still pursuing and growing. Avoid older company where discussions are on the past. It could be that the halfway mark of your life goals is the most dangerous place to be and at that point you need to refine them. Get alone again and study your target areas and embellish and improve some of the major goals. By now you have learned many lessons and gained insight into your own capabilities, so on the basis of where you have come from, you have a good idea of how much further you can go. Do not slacken or be seduced into some side issue.

On moving away from your charter you lose an appreciation for the business climate and associated events. Sometimes it is almost impossible to recapture lost ground.

**Pointers**
→ 1. *It is human to question what you are doing here.*

→ 2. *Be futuristic in your conversation and outlook.*
→ 3. *Associate with young, thinking, aggressive people.*

## A quantum jump

As we progress and achieve our goals and approach the object of our life goals, we need to reassess our assets in relation to the task left. Earlier, our ideals were obvious and our finances were restricted, but closer to the top life can become routine and we may lose that special feeling which makes us stretch and strive. In losing that, we are restricting the best years of our lives and our biggest potential.

Life at the top can have many distractions, and it is when you are popular and in demand you may confuse activity with objectivity. What a waste to let all of that ability continue at cruising speed when the engines are just run-in and ready for the race of a life time. In the previous section, I suggested it was necessary to stay on the track, but now I am encouraging you to take a quantum jump on that track. The reason I suggest such a bold move is that it will release all of that pent-up power into a constructive force which will realise the maximum amount of remaining potential.

A quantum jump could mean a doubling of your life goals or an increase on major goals — even an expansion of all remaining goals under new planning and strategy. But this time within tight time frames. A quantum jump means what it says: a big move forward. If you want some kind of guideline, you will need to make it large enough to get your conscious and sub-conscious attention and make you just a little bit scared so your total thinking process will be activated. A quantum jump does not mean gambling what you have achieved for double or nothing. Rather it means retaining what you have and securing it. Then, with new vigour and vision, you launch into an explosion of growth equal to, and not below, your abilities and time frames. It is now time to move into new directions of thought and energy which will act as a benchmark for others to follow. But best of all, it is you at your best, performing now more in harmony with your body, mind and spirit than you ever have before. You will probably find it will prolong your life and you will be happier with your work than you have ever been before.

### Pointers
→ 1. *A quantum jump creates energy.*
→ 2. *A quantum jump uses all potential.*
→ 3. *A quantum jump is not a gamble.*

## Treat other people with dignity

I was in a foreign country as a guest of the government and we were inspecting some irrigation schemes to assist the locals in growing crops. I asked my driver to stop and went into the fields to speak to a woman working with a hand hoe. When I spoke to her she responded by calling me, "Master." I don't think I have ever been so shocked as I was at that moment, and to this day I still feel the indignity that one human should be addressed that way by another. As I moved throughout that country I made sure I would never allow anyone to call me that again, and I would relate to everyone I met on an equal basis.

Well do I remember as a child some people who lived in a big house behind us who were to be treated as something more than human. We should remember that we all depart from this earth equal. I hear a lot of talk about being a good loser, but very little is said about being a good winner. To be a good winner is to treat people with dignity, respecting the right to proper courtesy and concern for others whoever they are. Many times in my life I have experienced help or encouragement from small courtesies, well in excess of that which I had given and at the most crucial time. Respecting others, in particular those who are not as well off as you, may be an encouragement to them to strive and better themselves. However, great care should be taken not to be condescending or artificial. Giving dignity to others gives dignity to yourself.

## Reaffirm your formula to others

As you progress and work on your life goals it will become quite obvious you have a formula that works. Give your formula to others so they in turn may grow. I have friends who continually send me new books, cassette tapes and magazine cuttings of things that they have found helpful, and in doing so they have doubled or tripled the value of their find.

*As you move through life, set aside good ideas and give them to others to encourage and inspire.* If you find somone who has gone broke or is having difficulties, share with them your own story of the difficult moments you faced and tell them about the formula you used in solving the problem. As you share your goals with others you reaffirm your own goals and gain additional emphasis and encouragement. Holding tight-fistedly to your newly-discovered plans and formulae to create growth and solve problems restricts us all.

## Give God the glory

As a Christian, I do not believe that we arrive by chance or by some accidental process of evolution over millions of years. I believe we were created by God for His glory and we remain here because of God's goodness. I fully accept the Bible as the inspired Word of God and without error in its original form. I believe that mankind is lost until we accept Jesus Christ as our Saviour in an act of faith. At that point we come under His grace and receive everlasting life. I further believe that our sojourn on this earth is full of opportunity to serve and to live out our convictions and participate in the joy of belonging to Christ. Any foolishness in this book I accept as my own, and for any wisdom included I give God the glory.